FS Books:
Sportsman's Best: Inshore Fishing
Sportsman's Best: Offshore Fishing
Sportsman's Best: Snapper & Grouper
Sportsman's Best: Sailfish
Sportsman's Best: Trout
Sportsman's Best: Redfish
Sportsman's Best: Dolphin
Sportsman's Best: Snook
Sportsman's Best: Kayak Fishing
Sportsman's Best: Sight Fishing

Sport Fish of Florida
Sport Fish of the Gulf of Mexico
Sport Fish of the Atlantic
Sport Fish of Fresh Water
Sport Fish of the Pacific

Baits, Rigs & Tackle
Annual Fishing Planner
The Angler's Cookbook
Florida Sportsman Magazine

Florida Sportsman Fishing Charts
Lawsticks
Law Boatstickers
Field Guide
ID Lawsticks

Author, Jeff Weakley
Edited by David Conway and Sam Hudson
Graphic Design by Mark Naumovitz, Drew Wickstrom

ISBN-13: 978-1-934622-50-6
ISBN-10: 1-934622-50-8

www.floridasportsman.com

 Find us on
Facebook

KAYAK
FISHING

CONTENTS

SB
SPORTSMAN'S BEST
KAYAK FISHING

12

110

144

172

210

188

The Kayak Fishing Journey

You're about to go on a ride from the inside of the world of kayak fishing—starting from powdery resin that rotomolded kayaks are made of in factories across the country, outward—out to fish some of the wildest places the vessels can take you along some of America's best river, lake, bay system and ocean kayaking locations.

On the way, Jeff Weakley's *Sportsman's Best: Kayak Fishing* will impart an intimate understanding of the variety of fishing kayak designs (and what waters and fishing they're best built for), their methods of construction (and with that, what these craft are truly capable of), how they can best be outfitted, repaired, and most importantly of all—how they're used and fished by experts on their home waters. You'll go on trips alongside some truly hardcore kayak anglers—from Seattle to Palm Beach, San Diego to Rhode Island.

You'll also get the deliverables. You'll get a breakdown—vividly illustrated with photos—of all the hardware. Included are the latest paddles, kayak pedal drives, fish bags, fishfinders, livewells, anchor systems, rudder systems, rod holders, trailer systems—and every other bit of gear and accessory that goes along with the ride. Read it before you rig up a new kayak and review it even if your present rig is outfitted to a T.

Jeff Weakley, Executive Editor of *Florida Sportsman magazine*, is one of the best all around anglers you could ever meet. From trolling offshore, to coastal flats fishing, to bass fishing on lakes and fly fishing for trout on mountain streams—he can do it all, but you wouldn't know that from this book—at first. That may sound strange, but Jeff is both a predator and an editor, and that's to your advantage as a reader. As an editor, he's tuned the technical fishing advice in the book to what's suited for kayak anglers in particular—and left out generic how-to info better suited for a general fisherman. Like an experienced kayaker, he's left behind all that you don't need to bring along on this journey to deliver what you do need for a revelatory understanding of where kayak anglers can go, what they can do and how they do it.

But Jeff hasn't done it alone. He's tapped knowledge from many of the leading authorities in kayak fishing—from manufacturers, to kayaking charter guides, to kayak shop owners from across the country—to present a composite picture of the state of kayaking today in the U.S.A. Jeff conducted countless interviews (okay, more than 50 at last count), and traversed the country over the span of a year's time to interview and fish with anglers in all kinds of waters—in addition to his own years as a kayak angler (Malibu Mini-X on his home waters of Stuart, Florida).

In the end, what you will have seen if you take the journey is some of the wildest life of all—the minds and hearts of the kayakers who have forged the sport of kayak fishing in our country, and those who are developing it further today. It's not history, but a live action story, put on paper, that's taking place right now. The members of the disparate patchwork of communities of kayak anglers all across the country—of which you are a part—all have much more in common with each other than they might at first suspect. A love of fishing, of setting forth on the water simply and quietly, of getting the heck away, and returning home safely from the adventure. This book affirms that shared desire and sets forth the myriad and all-enjoyable ways to pursue that passion.

David Conway,
Florida Sportsman Magazine

Sunrise on the no-motor-zone of a North Carolina lake.

Ever wonder what's on the other side? Come with us and let's find out.

Why Kayak?

Fishermen come to kayaks from many directions. The same may be said for the theory and process behind this one-of-a-kind reference book. Each chapter has been carefully researched and prepared to answer a variety of questions, and solve a range of problems, for kayak anglers.

Who, then, is the kayak angler? Some reading this book have been lured by the promise of newfound efficiency, a relatively inexpensive, low-maintenance ticket to open waters. Standing on shore over the years, one can't help wondering, What if I could just fish there? That open water beyond the breakers, that far shoreline with the tantalizing weed edge, that pond with the murky banks with little foothold. For a modest investment in capital and physical exertion, a kayak takes you there.

And then there is the fisherman who is a lifetime devotee of small boats. Perhaps a canoe, or a series of canoes, small outboard craft, wooden prams, has been in his personal fleet. This is the case for your present author, for many years a fan of double-bench seat canoes from which two anglers, or one intrepid paddler, may silently glide across crystal clear saltwater shallows. The difference between a canoe and a kayak is arguably very thin, and with each passing year the two grow closer to meeting. There are craft defined by their manufacturer as canoes which venture in design and utility very close to kayaks. And likewise kayaks which approach canoes. I'm speaking of course of so-called hybrid designs: Kayaks designed for the fisherman to sit inside the hull, elevated on a seat.

The canoe, mainly, is designed for one or more single-blade paddles—though many canoeists learn happily that a double-blade kayak paddle works well for propulsion. And yet a fan of canoes immediately recognizes the thrill of constant, straight-line motivation provided by the whirling blades of the kayak paddle. Like the shore fisherman, the owner of a canoe—or other cartopper—is attracted by the change in perspective.

Many powerboat owners find the kayak a perfect companion vessel, the "easy button," if you will, a no-hassle alternative to the DC systems, the thirsty gasoline engine, the expansive cleaning obligations demanded by a larger fiberglass hull. Unable to round up the necessary boat crew for a Saturday morning fishing adventure? Launch the kayak for a solo mission. Enjoy some exercise while you're at it.

Some kayak anglers relish the sense of kinship to the earliest outdoorsmen. Nimble, animal-skin kayaks were among the original vehicles of North American settlement. The desperately overloaded Niña, Pinta and Santa Maria came along much later. When you set forth in your paddle boat, you are delving into prehistory. It's sporting, in the way bow-hunting is to the deer hunter. Some fishermen take the concept to its logical pinnacle, constructing wooden kayaks by hand. Of course, there's no social penalty for fishing in rotomolded polyethylene craft.

And there are anglers for whom the kayak is a special-ops vehicle for surgical strikes into waters presenting a range of challenges. Silence—more than any fancy rod or lure, casting talent or confluence of conditions—is often the key to landing large fish in calm or clear waters.

Why Kayak?

With the range of experiences, predictably, comes a range of choices. Today there are dozens of kayak manufacturers producing paddle-driven boats from 8 to 18 feet in length. How might one decide on the right kayak? Making matters at once more exciting and more confusing, builders are integrating new modes of propulsion. Indeed one may kayak fish these days without reaching for a paddle. Pedal-driven kayaks free up the arms for day-long fishing. And the spectrum of accessories is bewildering. Just what is all that stuff used for?

An unspoken truth of kayak fishing, rarely addressed in online forums and clubs, is that because you are in a small boat, and close to the water, and relying on your own physical strength for propulsion, eventually you will enter the water against your wishes. You may lose a paddle. You will be caught by contrary weather. You will one day capsize—either on an early outing, or while freeing a snag, or while pushing the limits in rough water. Safety issues must be clearly addressed: The kayak fisherman must start with the minimum standards required by the Coast Guard and state authorities and proceed from there.

Outfitting and transporting kayaks for different situations is another topic of special interest to fishermen. What lies at the end of the road? A small lake with no improved launching facilities, or a concrete boat ramp followed by a miles-long paddle across open water? Will the kayaks be okay strapped to the rooftop, or will a trailer be more efficient? What of inflatable boats for flying across the country?

And of course, where will these vessels take us, and what sorts of fish might we encounter? While all the chapters in this book are bounded by the physical realities of paper and ink, this latter line of discussion leads the farthest beyond the pages. Nevertheless, *Sportsman's Best: Kayak Fishing* takes the reader on a vessel- and gear-focused tour of major fisheries in the continental United States. We look at the tackle and tactics needed to catch largemouth bass, spotted seatrout, saltwater bass, king mackerel and a wide range of fresh- and saltwater species.

Plus, we explore some of the sideways and byways of kayak fishing, including the new and related rage: standup paddleboards.

The only aspect of kayak fishing not covered herein, by choice, is whitewater. Anglers wishing to venture forth on the rough-and-tumble streams must begin not with a book, but with formal, personal instruction in sit-inside river boats—learning the proper strokes, how to roll the vessel, how to perform rescues in moving water. For that matter, authoritative kayak instruction is recommended for all, and we'll include contacts for instructors at the end of the book.

Within these chapters, and summarized toward the end of the book, are tributes to the flat-water kayak fishing lifestyle, with a few detours into the open sea. Learn where the sport may take you, the kinds of people you might meet, the kind of fisherman you may become.

Jeff Weakley, Author

What To Look For

Hook Points
Chapter Points

Seattle
Chapter 2

Great Lakes
Chapter 8

Rhode Island
Chapter 3

Santa Barbara
Chapter 12

Chesapeake Bay
Chapter 4

Aransas Pass
Chapter 9

Greensboro
Chapter 2 & 8

San Diego
Chapter 9

Panhandle
Chapter 14

Baja Peninsula
Chapter 12

Indian River Lagoon
Chapter 15

Tampa Bay
Chapter 11

West Palm Beach
Chapter 13

Sportsman's Best: Kayak Fishing is first and foremost a guide to selecting, outfitting and using a kayak for fishing. The principles covered in the following pages will be helpful to anglers anywhere, whether fresh water or salt, big waters or small. That said, we've made a thorough effort to deliver region-specific advice in a number of areas. The intent is not to serve as a travel guide, but rather to stimulate interest in kayak fishing, and showcase various applications for the gear and techniques described.

A substantial portion of the second part of the book, dealing with different types of waters, contains interviews and personal accounts relating to diverse fisheries. On the map, we indicate with a blue star those regions of the U.S. that are covered in the main body of the corresponding chapters.

Interwoven through the entire book are Hook Points, brief synopses of local fisheries of special interest to kayak anglers. These are noted on the map in the form of a red star.

Many of these places the author has personally fished; others are supported by interviews and photographs contributed by local experts.

Also keep an eye out for fish icons scattered throughout the book. These indicate summaries of popular species. Images and key details from the popular Sport Fish book series are coupled with kayak-specific advice.

CHAPTER 1

Your First Kayak

T he era of the kayak shop has arrived. Starting in the late 1990s, kayak fishing began evolving from a loose network of do-it-yourselfers sprucing up general touring boats, into a field every bit as specialized as bicycling, auto customization and power-boating. Dedicated kayak shops near popular fisheries typically carry the kinds of kayaks, paddles, and gear needed for that area, and staff are likely capable of performing repairs and upgrades. Online forums, of course, are a huge help for the new kayaker, but much good comes out of forging a relationship with a local retailer.

Dedicated shops near popular fisheries typically carry the kinds of kayaks, paddles and gear needed for that area.

The sense of discovery you'll enjoy with your new kayak should be shared with all of your family and friends.

Buying Your First Kayak

It's important to start with a fundamental understanding of hull design.

South River Outfitters typifies the family-owned kayak shop, a place where rentals are offered, guidance is provided, sales are made and dreams are realized. It's in Stuart, Florida, where I live.

Owner Ed Stout has been at this location, on the South Fork of the St. Lucie River, for 8 years. Like many kayak anglers, Ed got the fishing bug at an early age, and spent formative years wading. "One day, I realized I didn't have to get wet!" he said.

The basics, Ed explained: The longer the boat, the more distance you can travel in a shorter amount of time, and the more open water you can cover. For tighter areas, like small creeks and ponds, you might want a shorter boat.

"Typically," he elaborated, "I ask a customer, 'Where are you going to fish? What's the target? How much paddling experience do you have?'"

Kayaks are often sought and bought strictly on a price basis, by fishermen who have a very general idea of what they're looking for: This boat will fit on the back porch, or this one has rod holders, this doesn't. And yet, it's important to start with a fundamental understanding of hull design.

SOTs and SUPs at OEX. (That's sit-on-tops and standup paddleboards at Ocean Express, Sunset Beach, CA.)

This hull flares out on the sides to offer additional stability.

A U-shaped hull, offers optimal paddling efficiency, but may sacrifice some stability.

V-shaped keel entry of the hull will cut through waves, and the gentle flare should deflect spray.

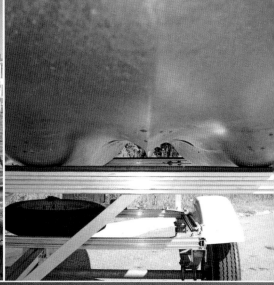

A tunnel hull, shaped like a "W," offers perhaps the best in terms of stability, but somewhat limited agility.

Wide, mostly flat bottom on Jackson Cuda promises stability. Entry vee at bow and stern helps with tracking.

The Language of Hull Design

Kayaks are described in the same terms as powerboats. There's a bow (front) and a stern (back), and beam (width) and length. There's a keel (bottom), chine (transition from gunnel to bottom). Additionally, rocker—or curvature of the keel from bow to stern—is also considered. For most flat-water fisheries, little or no rocker is best. It's the mountain whitewater boats that are rockered out to splash over falls and rapids. Some rocker is

also useful for kayaks used heavily in the surf.

Some kayaks are better suited than others for new paddlers. The term stability is of course relative, but when push comes to shove, so to speak, the wider hulls (beamier), generally speaking, offer better resistance to rolling. Even more, kayaks with concave or double concave bottom configurations—shaped like a W or a VW when viewed from the front or back—"shoulder out on either side, which is geared toward stability and ease of use," said Ed. He pointed to an Ocean Kayak on one of his racks, by way of example.

A U-shaped hull—in this case Ed showed a Wilderness Systems Tarpon model—is less stable, but more efficient (the company also offers twin-hull configurations).

Fishermen must therefore consider the tradeoff— the longer the boat, the more speed. "Actually it's better to talk in terms of efficiency," Ed clarified. "Speed has a lot to do with the paddler—a strong paddler can get a 'slow' boat to go fast, for instance." Basically, the greater the wetted surface area, the more friction, which equates to less speed for a given unit of effort. "Drop that boat in the water, look at every part that got wet—that's your wetted surface area," said Stout.

Fishing kayaks of 12 to 13 feet, about 30 inches wide, dominate the fishing circles, according to Ed and other retailers interviewed for this book.

On the other end of the spectrum, mini kayaks, 8- to 10-footers, are popular among anglers looking for lightweight, easily portable craft. Home storage is another factor—be sure you can successfully store your boat in your home or apartment.

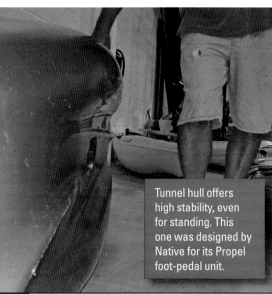

Tunnel hull offers high stability, even for standing. This one was designed by Native for its Propel foot-pedal unit.

Compact kayak that fits in the truck is handy for launching "on the fly." Below: Sebastian LaHara demonstrates a Heritage sit inside fishing kayak, also small enough to easily and efficiently launch in any desired location.

Sit On Top or Sit Inside?

A sit-on-top (SOT) kayak means just that: You sit on top of the vessel. The molding process produces a hollow-body kayak which is watertight (or mostly so, depending on how many rigging holes you drill in it). Water which splashes or runs onto the deck drains out through scupper holes, though not before possibly wetting you in the process.

Proper attire and different seat designs can minimize the "wet butt" problem of the SOT, but if personal comfort is more important to you than a self-draining boat, a sit-inside kayak may be a better choice, with some caveats.

Storage is another factor to consider. Be sure you can successfully store your boat in your home or apartment.

Whitewater kayaks are generally sit-inside designs, and their owners take them into some of the gnarliest water imaginable. But, these specialized boats are protected from water intrusion by spray skirts, and their paddlers must be expert in righting the vessel (rolling) in the event it overturns. Recreational and touring sit-insides may be enlisted for light fishing duties; they hold lots of gear, but again, they hold water. A hybrid kayak, open like a canoe, is another option for calm water, with greater storage capacity than the SOT. Kayaks outfitted or designed to accommodate raised seats may provide a more comfortable position for some anglers.

One important aspect of selecting a kayak is determining how easy it is to exit the boat

How much gear, how many rods? You decide Above, forward well on a Hobie Pro Angler gobbles up dry bags and other items. At left, center compartment on a Jackson Cuda swallows extra fishing rods.

(if you plan to wade), and more importantly, how easy it is to right it and climb back on if—make than when—you get dumped. You may find yourself attempting this critical manuever after asking yourself, of a prospective new kayak: Can I stand in this thing?

In Chapter 3 we'll look at accessory outriggers designed to add stability for standing. And there's even a 'yak that opens up into two pontoons, the Freedom Hawk. But, for the most part, few kayaks are really suitable for standup fishing. Those that are, are generally more than 34 inches in width. Standup paddleboards are treated elsewhere in this book.

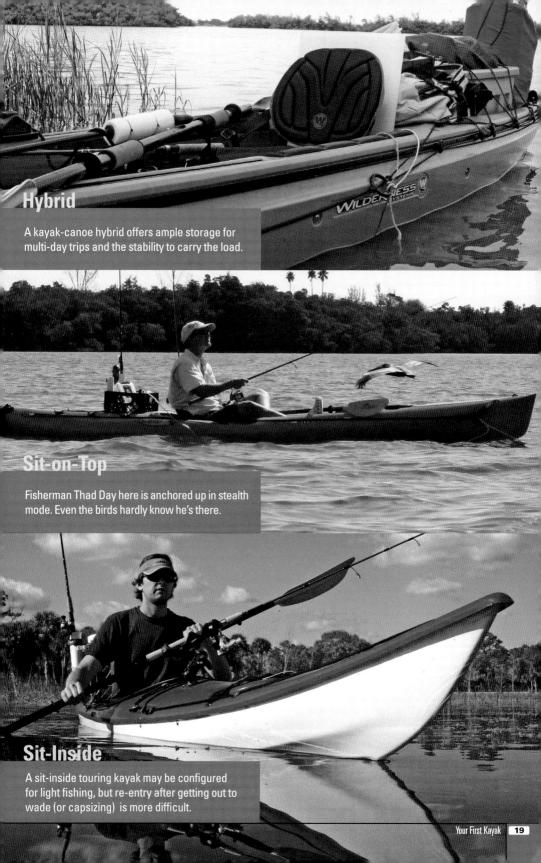

Hybrid

A kayak-canoe hybrid offers ample storage for multi-day trips and the stability to carry the load.

Sit-on-Top

Fisherman Thad Day here is anchored up in stealth mode. Even the birds hardly know he's there.

Sit-Inside

A sit-inside touring kayak may be configured for light fishing, but re-entry after getting out to wade (or capsizing) is more difficult.

The Test Run: Sit and Stroke

Trying out a kayak before purchase makes sense. Spend a little time on the boat to ensure the ergonomics are correct.

So trying out a kayak before purchase makes perfect sense, whether it's at a local retailer, a rental on the lake, or through an acquaintance made on the Internet or elsewhere.

Ed encourages potential customers to spend a little time on the boat, to ensure the ergonomics are correct, the paddling stroke easy and relaxed.

"If you overload the boat, it'll feel tippy," he said. "Or maybe you'll find that you must work harder, spending more time on corrective strokes. All boats are shaped differently, just as people are shaped differently."

On that score, the first and most important

more adjustable models, with features such as rod holders in the seatback, storage pouches, drink holders and more.

Of course, if the kayak will be used primarily as a short-duration conveyance to wading grounds, a high tech seat is beside the point. But for trips where you expect to paddle continuously for more than 30 minutes, the right seat, properly adjusted, can make a big difference, as in minimal lower back fatigue, less risk of chafing.

Of South River's inventory, Ed says the Wilderness Systems Phase III seat is "probably the most comfortable out there." It has recline adjustments on either side

Frame seat with adjustments and lumbar support may be the ultimate in fishing comfort.

(typical of most on the market), a seatback that can be raised or lowered, and a thigh-height adjustment.

The GTS seat is another one Ed noted for comfort. "It's really tall, with dual back adjustment supports, for the mid back as well as the high back."

Both seats come with accessory packs, which can clip to the back: dry bag, additional storage, water bottle and rod holders.

"The longer you're gonna be in the boat, the more important those accessories are," said Ed.

A seat material that attracts and holds water will feel cool to your skin, but after a while, you may want to dry out. Also, foam seats dry out quicker, but tend to rub skin less comfortably.

Hybrid kayaks and some sit-on-tops, such as the Native Watercraft Ultimate, Hobie Pro

kayak accessory (besides a PFD, which we'll cover later) is a seat, and here again, it's useful to try a few out in the shop.

Most kayaks are sold with accessory seats these days; that derriere-shaped bucket in a rotomolded boat is built to contain the seat, not the paddler. Try paddling a kayak with nothing to contain your backside, and you'll quickly find yourself fatigued.

Seat prices typically range from about $50 for the most basic seat, to more than $100 for

Angler and Jackson Cuda, feature lounge-chair style aluminum frame seats that elevate the paddler from his feet, not quite as high as a canoe, but pretty close. Anglers who suffer from stiffness in the lower back or knees, or don't feel comfortable sitting long periods with legs outstretched, may find these type seats more comfortable. These are also terrific in that they keep your butt out of the water!

Foot braces, typically sold as part of the package, may also be adjusted. Some kayaks, particularly the minis, feature molded-in spots to fit your feet. Most of the adjustable braces are pretty durable, though obviously the molded type have no chance of failure.

Kayak Paddles

Paddle selection falls under a similar governing principle as does the seat: for short trips, not much of a concern. A basic $59 paddle will get you to the same flat as a more expensive model. Just ensure that you match the correct length shaft with your height and the width of your kayak. Most are sold in 220, 230 and 240 centimeter lengths.

Most paddles have a label indicating the appropriate paddler's height, and the width of the kayak.

"You can start with aluminum shaft paddles," said Stout, "they're pretty light, but not as durable as the next step, fiberglass. Fiberglass paddles don't have to be rinsed, and they're stronger. You can get carbon and graphite paddles, which are really light; my lightest weighs 24 ounces. If you're holding on to the paddle 4 to 6 hours a day, seven days a week, that may be real important."

There's an array of blade sizes and shapes on the market, but it breaks down into two main families: Long and skinny, and short and fat.

"Short and fat paddles are used for high-angle stroke, when the paddle shaft is at a high angle in relation to the water," Ed explained. "That's a more powerful stroke; you'll move quickly but it'll take more energy. A low angle stroke, used with a long and skinny paddle, will move you slower, but over a longer duration."

An adjustable shaft is useful, one that can be locked into a couple of different "feathering" angles.

Feathering basically means the blades are twisted opposite to one another, so that as the propelling blade dips into the water, the elevated blade is slicing through the air. That minimizes resistance, which can help increase your water speed and range.

"I recommend starting unfeathered," says Ed.

Canoe vs. Kayak Paddle

At left is a basic canoe paddle: a single, mostly flat blade for upright, straight, forward-to-back strokes. The asymmetric kayak blade at right is cupped and contoured for optimal propulsion while being easy to swing through the water and the air overhead (remember there's a second blade waving against you in the air). Below is a view from under the surface.

Many kinds of paddles are available. At right, Jackson Big Tuna tandem fishing kayak.

"If you think you'll need to go faster, or are having problems with the wind, then feather the blades. But I tend to think most guys will have an easier time paddling with blades unfeathered."

A bent shaft paddle is another option, shaped somewhat like a curl bar in a gym. It's desiged to better align the wrist. "I've seen this help paddlers with wrist or elbow problems, even shoulder problems," said Ed.

On the subject of paddling strain, Ed said starting with proper technique is vital.

"Basically put the center of the paddle dead center on your head, and have your arms at 90 degrees; that's where your hands should be; some people put tape there. If your hands are out too far, you'll wear out your shoulders; in too close, it's a lever you'll work a lot harder."

Ed Stout shows proper hand placement on a kayak paddle.

Basic Stroke

Paddle blade should enter the water about even with your toes.

Using your hips and torso for leverage, pull the kayak forward.

Tandem 'Yaks

Double-seaters are fun for paddling with a child or significant other, but if you're planning to buy just one kayak, think long and hard before investing in a tandem.

Will your hoped-for partner honestly make time to join you? If not, you'll likely be paying more bucks for more weight, less enclosed storage space, and inconvenient paddling.

There are some scenarios where a tandem kayak makes very good sense, from a fishing standpoint. Gonzo anglers wishing to catch tarpon or other very large, powerful fish, may depend on a having a buddy on the boat to handle a paddle during the fight. Applying pressure to a big fish from a kayak is very difficult—a 100-pound tarpon can tow you

along for hours as if you were little more than a minor nuisance. Drift anchors discussed elsewhere in this book can help you hold your ground, but nothing works as well as a second guy paddling in reverse, or angling the kayak in the proper direction.

Also, if you have a very small vehicle and limited storage space at home, and your primary destination is a sandbar or other wading destination, the tandem kayak simplifies things to some extent. Two of you can go in one boat.

Kids? They'll go along wherever you put 'em. Little ones can sit between your legs for short trips. Or behind the seat, or on a forward seat such as the Malibu Gator Hatch. Big kids might like to sit in the tandem, but they might also prefer their own boat.

This paddler is just getting going; there'll be less disturbance on subsequent strokes.

Remove blade when your hand is about even with your hips, and repeat on alternate side.

Ship Without a Rudder?

If you've decided on a 12-foot-plus kayak, consider adding a rudder. And by consider, I mean inquire at the shop as to the particulars for installation. Making cable runs inside a rotomolded kayak can be very tricky. Fortunately, many newer models come with cable tubes installed.

The rudder offers two benefits. One, it helps the kayak track straight—meaning the vessel is less subject to lateral shifts with each paddle stroke. This little bit of added efficiency can ease those long trips. A rudder can also be used to help turn the kayak.

Shown here is a Harmony Blade Tracking System, an aftermarket kit offered by Confluence Watersports. The kayak is a Wilderness Commander 140—among the biggest of the rotomolded kayaks; a hybrid design; and a terrific gear hauler. Owner Mark Naumovitz (who supervised the art direction for this book) said the foot-pedal-adjustable rudder cut in half the number of strokes required to turn the 14-footer.

A rudder can also be used to adjust the drift angle of the kayak, a factor we'll discuss in greater detail in the Kayak Fishing Afloat (Chapter 9). SB

Rudder Installation

All of the necessary pieces come ready to go. Including rudder, sliding foot braces and hardware.

Start by removing the factory handle and replacing it with a bungee attached.

Install the rudder brace in the pre-molded threads with two allen screws and washers.

Slide the rudder into the rudder brace. It looks pretty good already doesn't it?

Drill holes (I know, heartbreaking) in the middle of the pre-molded holes.

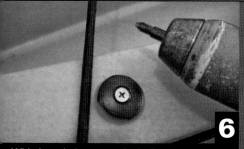

6

With those holes, screw in the hardware to help in running the rudder line.

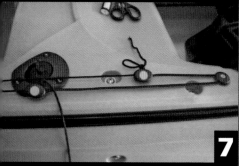

7

The rudder line should look something like this. Clean up the ends with scissors and lighter.

8

Run the steel cord (one on each side) in the rigging hole and crimp o-clamp to the end.

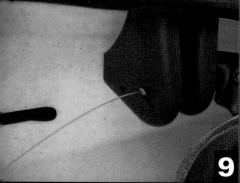

9

The other end of the steel cord ends up in front of the seat next to the foot braces.

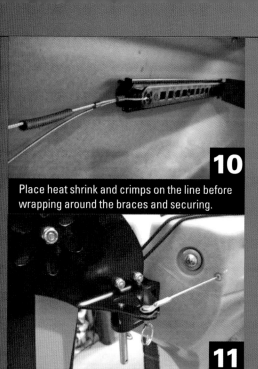

10

Place heat shrink and crimps on the line before wrapping around the braces and securing.

11

Test out the tension then place the o-clamps in place with pins once the slack is removed.

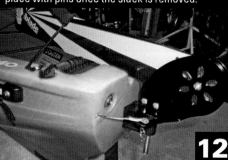

12

Test out the rudder by raising and lowering it with the rudder line. Then secure with bungee.

13

Time to hit the water! Enjoy the ability to maneuver your rig with fewer paddle strokes!

What's the best kayak for my kind of fishing? It's not an easy question. By no means exhaustive, here's a gallery of some sit-on-top kayaks built for fishing. For some of these vessels, you'll find further details and applications in subsequent chapters.

Bass Lake

Native Mariner 12.5 Propel

Length: 12 ' 6"
Width: 32"
Weight: 87 lbs.
Capacity: 400 lbs.
Notes: Pedal drive; stability and gear capacity for bass tackle needs

Open Bay

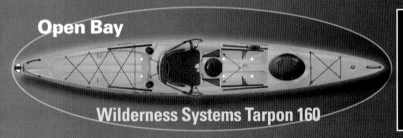

Wilderness Systems Tarpon 160

Length:16'
Width: 28"
Weight: 83 lbs.
Capacity: 375 lbs.
Notes: Cross open coastal water quickly

Open Bay

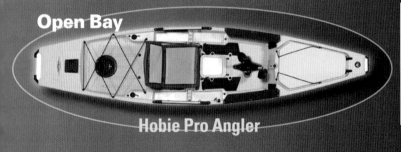

Hobie Pro Angler

Length: 13'8"
Width: 38"
Weight: 138 lbs.
Capacity: 600 lbs.
Notes: Pedal drive for range; stability for standup fishing

Fly Fishing

Jackson Cuda

Length: 14'3"
Width: 30.5"
Weight: 74 lbs.
Capacity: 400 lbs.
Notes: Molded rail and tip protector to safely carry fly rod; high/low seat

specs of selected sit-on-top kayaks for a variety of waters.

Wading

Malibu Mini X

Length: 9'3"
Width: 33.5"
Weight: 39 lbs
Capacity: 325 lbs.
Notes: Terrific size as a wading caddy (good surf boat, too)

Sea

Ocean Kayak Trident 13

Length: 13'6"
Width: 29.5"
Weight: 56 lbs.
Capacity: 450 lbs.
Notes: Designed and pre-rigged for rough water fishing

Standup

Diablo Adios

Length: 12'5"
Width: 36"
Weight: 69 lbs.
Capacity: 400 lbs.
Notes: Hybrid of standup paddleboard (SUP) and kayak

Standup

Freedom Hawk Pathfinder

Length: 14'2"
Width: 32"
Weight: 70 lbs.
Capacity: 375 lbs.
Notes: Unique split-hull for maximum stability

River

Jackson Coosa

Length: 11'2"
Width: 32"
Weight: 70 lbs.
Capacity: 375 lbs.
Notes: Creek-style rocker and stability for fishing moving water

CHAPTER 2

Design and Construction

We've looked at the basic types and specifications of fishing kayaks, and we have some idea of our needs. Before we begin outfitting a boat, let's digress for a moment into the fascinating and little-understood world of kayak construction. These simple vessels are the end result of a complex process, from conception, to modeling, to testing, to molding. If you understand how they're put together, you'll have a better appreciation for what makes a quality craft, and some insight into how to care for and outfit a fishing kayak.

Let's digress for a moment into the fascinating and behind-the-scenes world of kayak construction.

Kayaks are easy to maintain and repair. If you do kill one, contact the manufacturer for recycling options or find some other use for it, right.

Malibu
Paramount, California

Hobie Cat
Oceanside, California

Native Watercraft
Greensboro, NC

Florida Sportsman Office
Stuart, FL

One of my first thoughts, when I decided to write a book on kayak fishing, was, how exactly are these things put together?

While scheduling fishing trips all over the map, I made it a priority to visit some of the U.S. factories for kayaks.

At the three facilities I toured, I was impressed by how many human hands are involved. While the actual rotomolding can be overseen by a few technicians, the entire assembly line is far larger; downstream, there are workers applying hardware, soft goods and packaging. There are designers and marketing staffers; drivers and shipping logistics contacts. I spoke with dozens of workers in different divisions, and there was a common connection: Pride in their work. At the end of the day, these folks know that their products are destined to provide enjoyment for countless paddlers, all around the world.

Well-built, rotomolded kayaks age well, if they've been cared for: kept out of the sun, carried on wheels. When buying a car you'll always take the time to look under the hood. Granted, kayaks aren't in the same class, money-wise, but nevertheless it pays to inspect a kayak before purchase; that goes for new as well as used. Does the seat well feel solid when you press on it? Does the hull appear uniform, with no cracks or thin spots? Is the keel solid, with no evidence of dragging? What kind of warranty is included?

When pride of workmanship meets pride of ownership, it's a beautiful thing.

The vast majority of kayaks sold to fishermen these days are rotationally molded polyethylene.

A Native Watercraft kayak emerges from one of the company's rock-and-roll molding units.

Rockin' in the USA

The vast majority of kayaks sold to fishermen these days are rotationally molded polyethylene—one single piece of plastic. They are lightweight and durable, no-nonsense craft.

Yes, there are hand-made wood and fiberglass kayaks, but it's more likely your boat started out as a scoop of colored powder, drawn out of a big box like so much cake mix. The poly powder was dumped into an aluminum mold, the top fastened tight, and the mold placed inside a rectangular oven roughly the size of a small Winnebago. The mold turned round and round on its longitudinal axis, while that whole oven rocked back and forth. As the powder heated up, it became a gel which wanted to adhere to the hot aluminum ... but the constant agitation, all that rockin' and rollin', kept the gel moving around all the various turns. After about 45

minutes, workers extracted the mold and moved it to a cooling station. At just the right time, the mold was opened and voila, your boat emerged.

If it sounds impersonal and less artful than traditional boat-building techniques, don't be deceived: A lot goes into mastering the "recipe."

Also, you may be pleasantly surprised how many kayaks are rotomolded and outfitted right here in the United States, by highly trained teams of

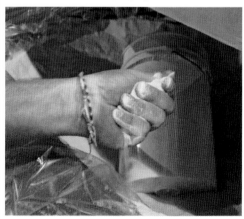

What your beloved kayak may at one time have looked like: powdered polyethylene resin.

After some time at the cooling station, the mold is separated and the finished kayak revealed, complete with logo and brass inserts.

workers who enjoy their jobs and take pride in their work. Behind the scenes are mad-scientist types constantly dreaming up new features, or testing materials and construction processes.

I toured three kayak manufacturing facilities to get a glimpse into this industry.

Legacy Paddlesports (parent company of Native Watercraft), in Greensboro, N.C., employs 80-plus persons working in three shifts. Woody Callaway is director of marketing, but has an extensive background in whitewater kayaking as well as kayak design and construction.

"Back in the '90s, we'd start with wood strips; we'd paddle it, add Bondo, make changes by hand," he explained of prototypes. "There's still a lot of hand work today, but pretty much the design work is done with computers—you have

> **There's a point where adding more plastic, you merely get more weight, without adding strength.**

an idea, you send the file to a guy with a 5-axis CNC machine; the plug comes back, we make a fiberglass mold of it, pull a part out of it. A fiberglass mold, it's going to last anywhere from 3 to 5 boats. We skim 'em out, let people check 'em out, give us their ideas.

"The hardest thing for a designer is taking feedback, fashioning questions to figure out what they're trying to say. You say you need more volume here, but the real question is: What's the boat doing that you don't like? It might not be a function of volume."

Even the final design, imprinted permanently in a heavy aluminum mold, is subject to adjustments. Kayak builders can use various applicants and air jets to draw more or less plastic to strategic points in the mold—thinner here, thicker here, as needed.

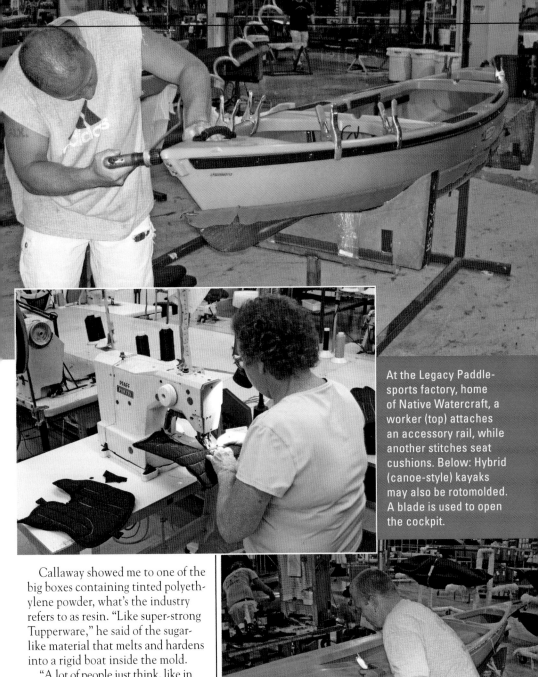

At the Legacy Paddle-sports factory, home of Native Watercraft, a worker (top) attaches an accessory rail, while another stitches seat cushions. Below: Hybrid (canoe-style) kayaks may also be rotomolded. A blade is used to open the cockpit.

Callaway showed me to one of the big boxes containing tinted polyethylene powder, what's the industry refers to as resin. "Like super-strong Tupperware," he said of the sugar-like material that melts and hardens into a rigid boat inside the mold.

"A lot of people just think, like in whitewater—'Well this hull broke, so we need to put more plastic in the hull.' But it doesn't work that way. Per weight and thickness, there's a point where the weight-to-strength ratio is high. But there's a point where adding more plastic, you get more weight, without adding more strength."

Rivet Replacement

1

Author broke an eyelet while surfing on his kayak (dumb). No sweat: He drills out the old rivet, using vice grips (smart!) to steady things.

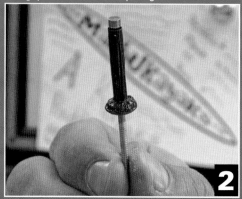

2

Local kayak shop furnished waterproof rivets, which can be used where screws can't get backing.

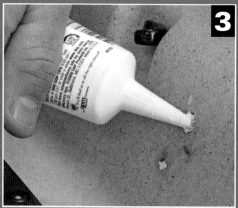

3

Silicon is a good universal, if not quite permanent, water sealer for any accessory attachments, including replacing an eyelet.

Kayaks are built to take some abuse, but those nylon eyelets and other accessories sometimes break. Here's a quick fixit.

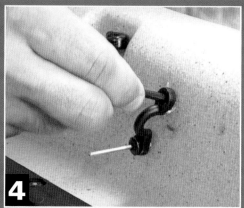

4

Set the eyelet on the beads of silicon, then insert the rivets. Now you're ready for the riveting.

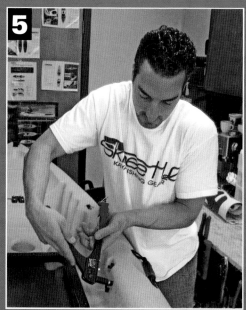

5

Sebastian LaHara, at Riverfront Kayaks in Jensen Beach, FL, finishes the repair job with a rivet tool.

Weeks after touring the Native factory, I spoke by telephone with Roger Geyer, technical and development director for Ravago, which produces the Aquatuf resin used by Native and several other manufacturers.

Geyer describes the material as a petroleum-based polymer, formulated specifically for roto-

> **It really is amazing to see a kayak come out, where minutes earlier someone was tossing colored powder into a metal coffin.**

Kayak makers at the Native Watercraft factory lift a kayak—fresh out of the oven—from its mold.

molding. Colorants and light stabilizers are added.

Native builds all its boats with Aquatuf 337—which Geyer says was developed for whitewater boats and other demanding applications. "It has a little more stiffness," he said, "noticeable when you climb into the canopy of a whitewater boat, for instance."

The Aquatuf 334 and 335 products are commonly used in touring or recreational kayaks.

Ravago works with manufacturers to field-test its products, sending boats crashing down rivers, over waterfalls.

Callaway took me to one of the big rock-and-roll ovens, where workers were just pulling out a mold. It really is amazing to see a kayak come out of one of those metal coffins, where minutes earlier someone was tossing colored powder inside. Every turn, every chine, every scupper—the whole boat is fully formed, just by that gel sloshing around inside the aluminum mold.

I saw essentially the same rotomolding processes in Paramount, California, at the Malibu Kayaks factory. Malibu President Sean Caples has distinguished his company by some novel design features, including a mid-tank oval livewell that sits between a paddler's legs. Also, the company offers a unique X-wing Sliding Console for electronics and other accessories.

"In the early 90s, when guys were pioneering the kayak fishing off Malibu," said Caples, "they were needing more than the market was offering—rod storage, livewells… and guys who fish, are often bigger guys, who need more stability."

Lately, among other projects, Caples and his crew (about 60 employees) have been obsessed with building a fully waterproof fishing kayak.

His look is So-Cal surfer, but Sean Caples runs a tight ship at Malibu Kayaks. At left: Hatch install. Bottom: X-wing Sliding Console.

"In the old days, many kayaks were outfitted with pop rivets, and these are points which can eventually leak," Caples said. "Today we're doing prescrewed eyelets, molded right into the boat."

Hobie Cat, a bit down the coast in Oceanside, California, also integrates fasteners and other non-structural components into the rotomolding process, as does Native. Each company has its own tricks; some of them I saw, but promised to keep secret.

Native, for example, figured out an ingenious way to mix colors, producing camouflage kayaks. I can't tell you how they do it, but the result sure is neat!

All of the manufacturers I visited demonstrated special attention to environmental conditions at the factory sites. If a hot polyethylene kayak comes out of a mold and rests in a rack exposed to chilly air gusting in on a winter day, for example, it can warp. Maintaining consistent temperatures in the factory, and adjusting the heat and timing of the ovens, is a mix of art and science which successful kayak manufacturers are constantly on top of.

Rudders and other accessories are installed on hulls molded at the Hobie Cat factory in Oceanside, California.

Jim Czarnowski, Director of Engineering for Hobie Cat, allowed me a glimpse into a shaping bay, where a man was working on a foam plug built for the company's new Revolution 11 kayak.

"That's basically a work of art," Czarnowski said, "all hand-done, in fiberglass, Bondo, gel-coat. We make the plug, and then send it to the mold maker, and they cast the aluminum mold."

"We'll test 100 versions of it... test, modify, back and forth to the ocean tons of time. We'll fish out of it, and once we're happy, scale it up and make the final version."

Hobie Cat has a long, colorful history of building watercraft, of which kayaks are only the latest iteration. In 1950, Hobie Alter built his first balsa wood surfboard; then the first fiberglass surfboard with polyurethane foam core (1958); then twin-hulled sailing vessels, in the late 1960s.

Sean Caples, on the other hand, came to the kayak industry somewhat late in the game, and then sort of tangentially. Malibu Kayaks came together in 1999 after Caples—who was running a retail shop in the epony-mous California beach

town—hit a sort of creative critical mass. He saw the kinds of boats people were taking fishing, the milk-crate improvised tackle containers. The classic entrepreneur, Caples parlayed his incipient, if not formally trained, interest in drafting and mechanical design into a successful kayak business.

"There's a lot of satisfaction in this business," he said. "When people email me to say they just had the best time, and they explain their day, that's cool to hear."

Hobie Mirage Drive assembly at the Oceanside factory (more on this system in the next chapter).

Repairing Poly Hulls Step-by-step guide to fast fixes

How tough are rotomolded polyethylene kayaks? Pretty darn tough! Here, Ed Stout at South River Outfitters—6-foot, 5 inches tall!—drops a cinderblock on an Ocean Kayak. The impact leaves barely a scratch.

If your significant other gets mad and takes an axe to your yak, the laceration may be repaired using a stick of polyethylene obtained from the manufacturer. (Sneak tip: If you drill out any large holes for rod holders or access panels, keep the leftover material—it, too, can be used to repair your boat.)

Heat gun has been fitted with a reducing nozzle to direct the energy toward the poly and the crack, much like soldering. Heat just until the poly is wet and conforms to the crack. Smooth it over with a metal tool immediately.

Another scenario: You've drilled in the wrong spot for an installation. Small holes like these are simple to repair.

Dragouts on the bottom of the hull are another story: Continually wearing away the keel of a kayak by dragging it across rocks or shells will eventually leave a long streak of thin-

Don't try this at home. Ed Stout (pictured) had a freight-damaged kayak, and I had a mission: see what these boats can handle.

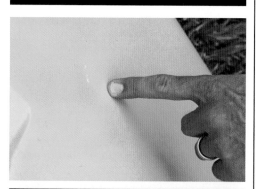

The cinder block produced a tiny abrasion, nothing more. "Hey Ed," I asked, "Got anything else?" He found something . . . an axe.

ning, cracking hull. This can be difficult if not impossible to fix. Some newer kayaks are being sold with extra-heavy or replaceable keel parts.

Always make it a practice to carry or wheel your kayak to and from the water.

(And try to keep axes and angry people away from your boat!)

Polyethylene repair stick is warmed with a heat gun. We chose blue for illustration.

Heat and apply the softened poly to the damaged area, then quickly flatten with screwdriver or other tool.

Definitely don't try this—you could end up splitting your forehead in the process! Anyway, we hacked a nice gouge in the hull.

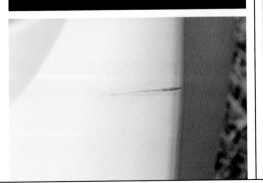

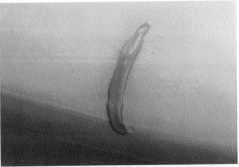

If the color matched, repair would be indistinguishable. Similar procedure for drill holes.

Pacific Northwest

Joe Kaftan, a fan of sit-inside hulls, instructs on weekends at Kayak Academy in Washington.

The sit-inside sea kayaks favored by many anglers on the Northwest coast are built from different manufacturing processes than the majority of the boats featured in this book.

Out in places like the Puget Sound in Seattle, Washington, speed and efficiency are favored over things like stability and rod storage. Full-coverage from the elements is also high on the list. The salmon runs are seasonal, mostly June through September, and bottom fish destinations can be far from urban areas. A typical sea kayak route might run 10, even 15 miles. In the hands of a capable paddler, the long, narrow kayaks slice through the water at speeds to 4 or 5 knots.

Joe Kaftan, a Seattle-based graphic designer and part-time kayak instructor, has an interesting background in cold-water kayak fishing: Lake Michigan in earlier years and more recently, the Pacific Northwest, including forays up to Vancouver Island and as far as Alaska. He's also familiar with the touring mindset—spending multiple days covering miles between beautiful islands—and the racing mindset, bolting across placid sounds in competition with other paddlers.

"Out here, sea kayaking is a lifestyle," he said. "People regard a fishing rod as an accessory to go with a kayak, not like Florida or southern California, where the kayak is an accessory that goes with the fishing rod."

When Kaftan fishes, more often than not it's out of a Prijon Kodiak (shown left and above), 17 feet in length, just under 24 inches in width—a totally different animal. Often times he'll troll a diving plug or a spoon behind a lead, holding the rod in his life jacket; others days he'll drop baits for cabezon, kelp greenling or rockfish. Hauling up crab traps from the kayak is another gastronomically pleasing diversion.

The Prijons are built in Germany through an extrusion and blow-molding process, wherein pellets of high-temperature plastic, or HTP, are squeezed in an extruder until they form a sticky substance,

which is then pressed through a die to form a tube (much like nylon monofilament fishing line is made!). A two-part mold bears down over the tube, and then air compression inside pushes the plastic into the shape of the mold. Water around the tube cools the form. Out pops a kayak.

Russ Cowles, eastern distributor for Prijon kayaks in Williamsport, Pennsylvania, said the process takes about 12 minutes—faster than the rotomolding described in this chapter. The key difference, he said, is the nature of the raw material, the HTP plastic.

"You can't rotomold it—if you heated it up in a rock and roll oven, it would never melt; it would turn into a big gumball. It's more dense and harder [than rotomolding polyethylene]."

The Prijon hulls, characteristic of sea kayaks, are light for their length. Shoulder-weight of a 12-footer, said Cowles, may be 42 pounds, which is about half what a full-beam rotomolded sit-inside might weigh.

Sit-inside sea kayaks and spray skirts necessitate competence in rolls and re-entry techniques not covered in this book. It's an exciting approach, but like whitewater kayaking, qualified training is vital.

More Than One Way to Skin a 'Yak

"The thing I like best about building my own fishing kayaks, is that I can make a kayak to fit me and my needs," reported Ed Mashburn, a teacher and writer residing on the eastern shore of Mobile Bay, Alabama.

"How strong are wooden kayaks? I've had kayaks I built slide out of the back of my truck as I drive down the road, and survive.

"Along with the great strength, wooden kayaks are light in weight. My 12- and 14-foot wooden kayaks weigh less than 40 pounds, and they paddle easily and maneuver well.

"There are a number of sources for kayak plans, but the one I use most is Guillemot Sea Kayaks; the Auk model converts very well into a fishing kayak." SB

Ed Mashburn of Bay Minette, AL, reported on this kit kayak build in *Florida Sportsman*.

CHAPTER 3

Push, Pedal, Power and Mor

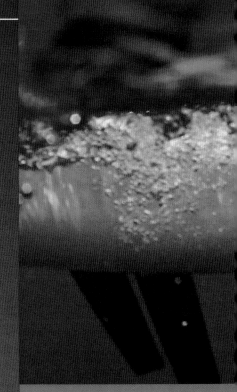

Now that you know the basics of kayak hulls, ergonomics and construction methods, let's look at some of the alternate propulsion systems. Hobie and Native Watercraft have made waves in the paddle-fishing world in recent years, with the development of foot-pedal-driven systems. The two companies, as well as Ocean Kayak, have also introduced electric motor kits. And there are all sorts of possibilities on the horizon, from sailing kits to solar-powered chargers. Will adding a motor change the registration requirements for your kayak? What are some fishing techniques we might explore using these new systems?

Now that you know the basics of kayak hulls, ergonomics and construction methods, let's look at some of the alternate propulsion systems.

Models of efficiency:
Hobie Mirage Drive (twin
black propulsion fins
visible opposite) and a
yellowfin tuna.

A Foot in the Door

The development of Hobie's Mirage Drive ranks among the great "Aha" moments in recent boating history.

With each cycle of the foot pedals, submerged fins move back and forth beneath the boat, propelling it forward with surprising speed and efficiency.

Mechanical engineer Greg Ketterman came up with the design in 1997, after ruminating on, and finally connecting, a couple of observations:

Greg Ketterman, left, invented the Mirage Drive for Hobie. The chain-driven wings "flap" like penguin wings and provide surprising thrust.

One, that leg power is naturally stronger than arm power, and two, that penguins swim awfully fast.

The first working prototype, Greg and his brother tested in the nearest waterway, Oceanside Harbor. Though the first fins seemed too big and the pedal resistance too much, Greg said, "We knew we had something."

Ketterman is a graduate of California Polytechnic Pomona. Before working for Hobie Cat, he worked a few years designing satellites for an aerospace company. The Mirage Drive he terms his "second baby." What's the first? The famous Hobie Cat Trifoiler sailboat, which will go 40 mph over the water. A competition model still holds the speed record, 52 mph.

The Mirage Drive system, as Ketterman explains it, is "analogous to the way penguins propel themselves."

"Two keys to an efficient propeller are twist, and ideally, the fin needs to have positive camber," he noted. "With each change of stroke, these fins are changing their camber and twist, to assume a good propeller shape."

The Mirage Drive actually improves on nature, as it creates as much propulsion on the up-stroke as it does on the downstroke. The humble penguin

Maximum draft is somewhere around 16 inches, but shorter strokes can swing the flippers in a little less than a foot of water.

Foot propulsion is especially useful when targeting large, powerful fish such as this jack.

has relatively weak back muscles, only used for returning each flipper into position for the next down-stroke powered by breast muscles.

The drives are built at Hobie Cat's factory in Oceanside, with stainless steel chains and cables, and engineering-grade nylon.

What happens to those flippers in very shallow water? Cool trick: You simply pull back on a pedal, and the two flippers fold up tight to the bottom of the hull. Maximum draft underway is somewhere around 16 inches, but shorter pedal strokes can effectively swing those flippers in a little less than a foot of water.

The other pedal-drive propulsion system on the market is the Native Propel.

As Native Watercraft's Woody Callaway explained

Pushpole Glide silently over the flats, watching for fish.

If your kayak is wide and stable enough to support you while standing, you might invest in a short pushpole or paddle/pole combo. It's perhaps the oldest mechanism in the history of boating: You simply drive the boat forward by planting one end of the pole in the bottom and pushing.

Several companies make suitable devices. Native Watercraft has a 9½-foot, 4-piece Paddle Pole with two different tips. At one end is a point, much like on a traditional flats skiff pushpole.

This can be used to push off on hard bottom, or anchor the boat temporarily in softer substrate. At the other end is a long, narrow blade, which may be used to paddle, steer or push.

Stiffy, a longtime manufacturer of powerboat pushpoles, offers a complete line of kayak and canoe poles. Fiberglass models from 5 to 12 feet are affordable and useful, with a spike at one end and a triangular "mud foot" at the other.

Many other systems are available.

First, you'll need a pushpole and a kayak that's wide and stable enough to support you.

In soft bottom, plant the Y-shaped end of the pole a little behind your heel.

Simply "walk" the boat forward, hand-over-hand, then pick up the pole and do it again.

The "mud foot" of a pushpole. Many models also have a metal "rock point" at the other end.

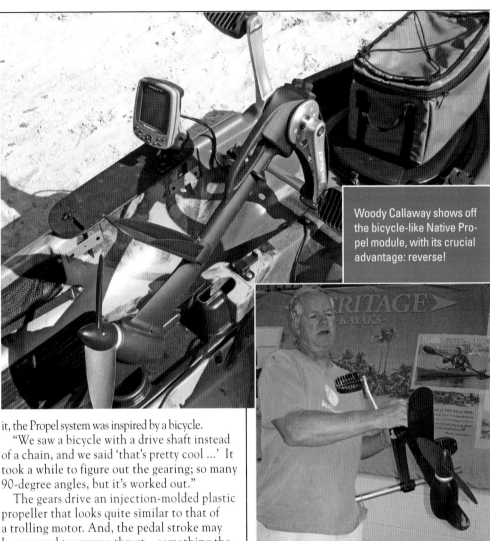

Woody Callaway shows off the bicycle-like Native Propel module, with its crucial advantage: reverse!

it, the Propel system was inspired by a bicycle.

"We saw a bicycle with a drive shaft instead of a chain, and we said 'that's pretty cool ...' It took a while to figure out the gearing; so many 90-degree angles, but it's worked out."

The gears drive an injection-molded plastic propeller that looks quite similar to that of a trolling motor. And, the pedal stroke may be reversed to reverse thrust—something the Hobie system is unable to do.

"We took this down to Florida, and filmed guys pulling snook out of the mangroves, big reds. You can hold your ground, keep them in front of you."

While researching this book, I had the opportunity to use both the Hobie Mirage Drive and Native Propel. Both were easy to operate.

Difficult to say which system works best, as the two companies integrate the drives into a wide range of craft—and the systems are only compatible with their respective manufacturer's boats.

The Hobie Pro Angler, for instance, is a sit-on-top kayak 38 inches wide, weighing 138 pounds. With the Mirage Drive, a reasonably fit person may pedal for 2 miles at a pace

which my personal (albeit unscientific) observation indicates is a bit faster, and less taxing, than a paddle stroke.

The Native Mariner 12.5 Propel, one of the company's popular fishing models equipped with the bicycle-style drive, weighs in at 87 pounds and 32 inches wide. It, too, made ground at a surprising clip under leg power.

Both of these systems are steered by hand-controlled aft rudder, similar in function to that shown at the end of Chapter 1

Sadly, I didn't have a chance to race the two: One was in San Diego Bay, California, the other a North Carolina reservoir.

Electric Motors

An electric motor on a kayak? Doesn't that make it a powerboat?

Well, in the eyes of most state motor vehicle departments, it does.

In nearly all circumstances, the moment you bolt a motor to a kayak, whether powered by 12-volt current or gasoline, you're obliged to abide by powerboat titling and registration forms and fees. Consult your own state DMV for specifics. Some states, including Florida, have exceptions for motorized vessels used exclusively on private ponds or lakes, meaning you could use an unregistered, motor-powered 'yak on a ranch pond, but not a public waterbody.

The Torque can make a normally hard day of paddling, quite enjoyable.

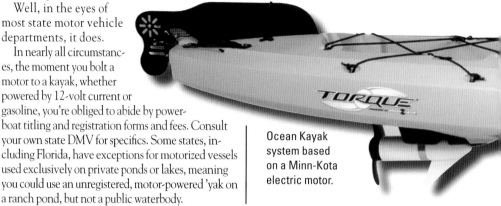

Ocean Kayak system based on a Minn-Kota electric motor.

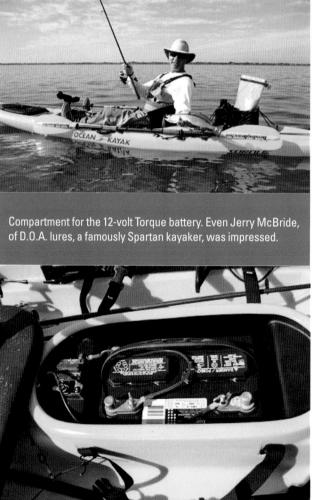

Compartment for the 12-volt Torque battery. Even Jerry McBride, of D.O.A. lures, a famously Spartan kayaker, was impressed.

If you do wish to add a motor, or buy a kayak with an integrated motor, such as the 13-foot Ocean Kayak Torque, you'll need to retain the receipt for sale and ensure you're provided a Manufacturer's Statement of Origin. These and perhaps other documents will be needed to fill out the paperwork at your local tax collector's office.

What might be some advantages to power? In the case of the Torque model mentioned, the 12-volt Minn-Kota motor works in forward or reverse. Not only can you scoot hands-free across the lake, you can back away from structure if you hook a big fish. The modular motor, weighing 20 pounds, drops into an aft well. The battery goes into a forward well, with circuit breaker. The motor then plugs into outlet on the boat. A control knob forward of the seat gives you Minn-Kota's "infinitely variable" speed control in forward or reverse—that means you can tune the motor down to a quiet, very slow level if creeping up on a fishing area, or accelerate as needed.

Solar-Powered Kayaks?

They might be coming to a watershed near you! Sea Eagle, longtime builder of inflatable kayaks and other small boats, introduced the Green Machine Fast Track kayaks at the Miami Boat Show in 2012.

The rugged, two-seater inflatables (a 12- and a 15-footer) are outfitted with an aluminum motor mount behind the rear seat. The mount carries a 1-horsepower Torqeedo electric motor and the Torqeedo 320-watt lithium ion battery. Together, the motor and battery weigh just over 15 pounds. A fully charged Torqeedo on a Fast Track may deliver speeds up to 8 mph, according to Sea Eagle.

At the bow is a flexible Power-Film Solar Panel, about the size and weight of a bath towel. Under optimal sunlight, the panel delivers 23 watts, enough to propel the Fast Track kayak at about 3 mph indefinitely, with surplus power for charging the battery (of course wind and tide must be accounted for).

The solar panel may also be used merely as a passive charger, while paddling the Fast Track or using the proprietary downwind Quik Sail.

The manufacturer estimates it'll take most owners about 8 minutes to inflate and assemble a Green Machine Fast Track.

This interesting little kayak runs on wind or solar power. Not something you see every day, but in the years to come, you may.

Under optimal sunlight, the panel delivers enough watts to propel the Fast Track at about 3 mph indefinitely.

You may be obligated to abide by powerboat titling and registration forms and fees. Consult your state DMV for specifics.

Trolling for Rhode Island Stripers

One of the many fishing applications for electric power on a kayak is a hands-free thrust-assist for hauling big fish away from trouble spots.

Bob Oberg, of Warwick, Rhode Island, is a fanatical striped bass fisherman. He puts in long hours, often under starry skies in remote waters, targeting his favorite fish at the optimal tide. Oberg's preferred technique is trolling a tube-and-worm combination deep on lead core line. It's a slow-spinning, throbbing, scent-emitting presentation that's deadly on big stripers. (Florida anglers might recognize the forward half of the combo as a

> "I'm typically trolling at 2 to 2.2 mph, with the bait 1 to 2 feet off the bottom."

Hobie eVolve motor is based on the Torqeedo system mentioned on the preceding page.

single-hook barracuda tube—Oberg custom-builds his own lures, but ready-made rigs are available in local shops such as Ocean State Tackle.)

"We have a big population of bluefish up here, and if you don't want to catch them, they're generally just above the stripers in the water column," he explained. "To catch the striped bass, I stay about 1 or 2 feet off the bottom. I'm typically trolling at 2 to 2.2 mph; with the 36-pound-test leadcore, if I'm fishing in 5 to 8 feet of water, I'll probably have about 45 feet of line out. I'll let more out, or take some in, based on what the conditions indicate."

The lead core line comes in colored sections for reference, 30 feet for each color. Using a Garmin GPS/fishfinder combo, Oberg zeroes in on precise depths. To detect bites or weed snags, he holds the fishing rod in his lap, while working the Mirage Drive pedals or the Torqeedo-designed eVolve motor on his Hobie Outback.

"Places I like to fish are often just outside where the waves are breaking, and a big fish will usually try to pull me into where they're breaking," Oberg noted. "I've learned that I can use the motor while fighting fish—the control is near my reel hand; I can control the speed, and curve the boat to slightly deeper water, even curve around to a full turn to fight fish from a more comfortable distance."

Oberg says the Torqeedo motor and battery have been dependable, and the computer controls surprisingly accurate. Some of his jaunts in Narragansett Bay may cover 15 or 16 miles, and so he brings a spare battery. "If I'm fishing one spot and want to gun it a mile to another spot, I don't worry about it."

"One thing that's really neat is the computer calibration of battery life is very accurate. If you cut back from 3 mph to 2 ½, for instance, you can add a lot of time."

Oberg's biggest striper to date was a mammoth 47-pounder, 49 inches in length. He caught the fish around 9 p.m. on a tide change in late September 2009, a day after the full moon. The fish struck a tube-and-worm in 5 feet of water in a secluded, oceanside cove. Oberg is a lifelong angler and resident of Rhode Island, and works as a development director for a non-profit organization helping raise money for low-income kids to attend college. He began kayak fishing in 2004, and maintains a fastidious logbook of striped bass behavior.

Bob Oberg lives a sort of double-life. By day he's a development director for a non-profit; by night a hard-charging kayaker on his Hobie Outback. That's a 47-pound striped bass.

Sport Fish for Kayakers

Yellowtail
(Seriola lalandi)

◆**A.K.A.** Pacific Yellowtail, Pacific Amberjack

◆**Range:** British Columbia to Panama, but common only from southern California southward.

◆**Size:** 15 to 30 pounds average. World record 114 pounds, 10 ounces

◆**Diet:** Squid and finfish

◆**Kayak Tactics:** Slow-troll or drift live bait such as mackerel or scad, especially around kelp beds and rocky dropoffs. Also watch for surface-busting fish, which are likely to bite a surface-swimming iron or plug.

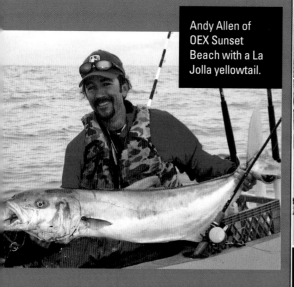

Andy Allen of OEX Sunset Beach with a La Jolla yellowtail.

Stabilizers

If you're going to do a lot of standup fishing on a kayak, you might research the compatibility of a pontoon stabilizer setup with the model you're looking at. Shown below is a stabilizer kit from Spring Creek Outfitters, based in Mountain Iron, Minnesota. Also shown on this page is the Hobie Adventure Island kayak/sail boat, with the company's proprietary "amas," or retractable outriggers.

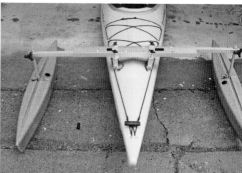

Outriggers on Hobie Adventure Island permit standup fishing, even in the sea. At top: Aftermarket outriggers from Spring Creek.

Sails

Adding a sail to a kayak is tricky, as there is no keel or centerboard to offer the lateral resistance needed for upwind sailing. A simple downwind sail, as shown on page 49, is feasible.

Hobie cracked the code with its MirageDrive pedal system: When the fins are in the down position, they act as a centerboard, allowing the vessel to sail upwind. The system also has a hand-control rudder. Shown here are a couple of different Hobie Cat models under sail power.

The Hobie Sailing Kit weighs just over 4 pounds, and includes a 10-foot mast, 20-square-foot sail, and all the necessary lines and hardware. It's compatible with all Mirage kayaks. SB

Breezing it up on a Hobie Mirage kayak with the optional sailing kit: solo, at right, or tandem, below. At top, Tandem Island series comes with its own larger sail.

When the Mirage fins are in the down position, they act as a centerboard.

CHAPTER 4

Accessories

Kayak fishing tends to attract spirited, do-it-yourselfers quick to build their own gear when situations demand it.

Some years ago, when I discovered the joys and challenges of trolling off Atlantic-coast beaches, I recognized the need for a small, short-handled gaff. I wanted it to perform different duties: Subduing eating fish, and reaching out to disengage the hook on jacks, bonito and other sport fish. In typical kayaker style, instead of going to a store, I went into my garage, cut a piece of heavy wooden dowel, whipped a 10/0 forged trolling hook to the end with cotton line, epoxied the wraps, and made myself what a charterboat mate would immediately recognize as a "cherry picker."

Its utility for sticking mackerel is obvious, but I find I use the hook more often to release fish. Forget about restraining a crazy jack or bonito: Simply grab the leader, catch the bend of the hook with the gaff, and lift—out pops the lure, away goes the fish. When the picker is secured alongside in a triangle paddle keeper, a piece of pool noodle or a tennis ball squeezed on the point keeps me from harm's way.

It doesn't look fancy, but it does the job.

Kayak fishing tends to attract spirited, do-it-yourselfers quick to build their own gear when situations demand it.

What you can't find in a shop (dude, really?!), you build yourself, as Florida angler Greg Timmer did with this 12-volt power source for a small fishfinder.

Anchors and Brakes

Guys who fish the kelp beds of California have a convenient means of holding fast—they simple grab a stalk of kelp and wrap it around a line affixed to the kayak.

Those of us fishing open waters in the rest of the country aren't so lucky.

In shallow water, to 4 feet or so, a staking anchor is very handy. Years ago, many guys jammed a busted-off golf club through a scupper to stay put. The Stick It pole, made in Florida, comes in 5 ½, 7- and 8-foot sizes; it sits in a paddle park alongside the vessel when not in use. Crack of Dawn and other manufacturers offer similar devices.

Ingenious method for handling anchor rode: A Christmas tree light reel! At left, PVC stake anchor.

Another alternative is a piece of 1-inch PVC with the end sawed off at a 45-degree angle, so that it can be driven into soft sand, mud or marl. I made one of these about the

This is an anchor trolley, or shuttle. The rope for the anchor or drift chute goes through the ring at left.

Pulling on the halyard, which runs through a pulley, moves the guide ring back and forth, to position the kayak optimally .

Drift chute fills up with water and adds drag to the kayak.

Rod Holders

Nowadays, most rotomolded fishing kayaks come from the shop or factory with at least a pair of flush-mount gimbal rod holders, usually behind the seat. For many anglers, that's entirely adequate. Your author, in fact, has long resisted the urge to install additional rod holders in his sea kayak, mainly to minimize leak-points in the boat.

There are many sources for flush-mount rod holders, but for raised systems, or specialized shapes for cradling fly rods or trolling outfits, Scotty and RAM offer a variety of solutions.

Ram

ame time I made my kingfish gaff—my PVC take is 9 feet long. Why so long? Docklight fishing in deep water, I found the need to take out so that I could pressure snook and rout out of barnacle-encrusted pilings.

Mushroom anchors or grapnels are useful n deep water. To safely deploy an anchor nd adjust it to suit the conditions at hand, nost kayakers use some form of anchor trol-ey. A stainless ring on a nylon halyard, with ulleys at bow and stern, is one solution. A air of line chocks or an S-cleat holds fast he anchor rode. You can move the ring, and he anchor rode, by pulling on the halyard. This is also a good method for handling the ollapsible drift anchors.

Drift chute, sea anchor, drogue—they go by lots of names. Handy for slowing the drift.

Scotty

Flush Mount Rod Holder Install

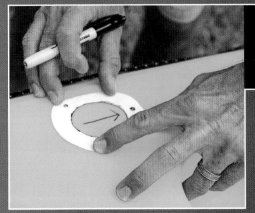

For a permanent rod holder, first carefully mark where it will go (template is used here), and at what angle. Ensure clearance belowdecks.

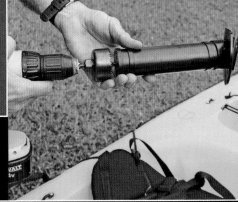

Hole saw bit sized appropriately to the belowdecks shaft of the rod holder.

Shown left, make a pilot hole straight overhead.

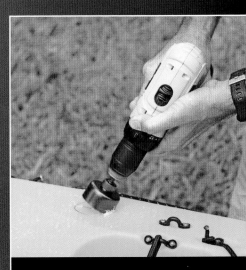

Now angle the bit at the correct angle.

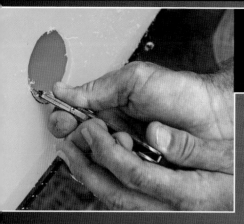

Clean up the hole with a sharp blade.

Place the part and drill out the rivet holes. This rod holder came with a rubber gasket and cap, to make it watertight.

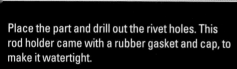

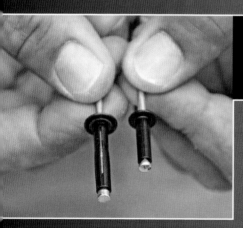

Longer rivet at left is the better of the two. It's a blind rivet which splits into three wings that hold fast inside a kayak. Buy from a kayak shop.

Rivet tool pulls up the metal stem, which causes the plastic anchor to flare inside the hull.

Sneak tip: Retain the disc of plastic you cut out. It may be used to heat-weld damaged spots later.

Crates, Tackle Boxes

You don't see as many kayakers these days toting around gear and rod holders in plastic milk crates bungeed in place. Kayak and accessory manufacturers have integrated all sorts of solutions into their products, from rod holders to dry storage compartments.

Another reason you don't see as many milk crates is, anglers are disguising them with cleverly designed utility bags. One such accessory is the Precision Pak Crate Pak, a self-draining polyester cover that has 3 rod holders, a stern light holder, and D-rings for securing to the kayak. It fits over a standard milk crate, approximately 12 inches by 12 inches by 15 inches.

A water-resistant backpack is another solution.

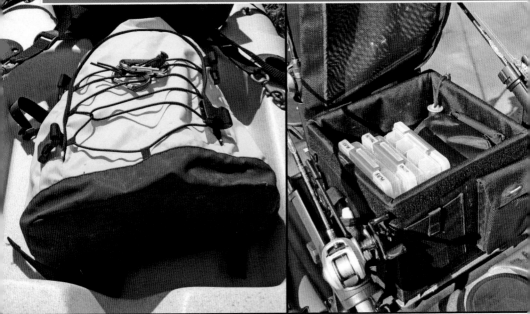

Top right is a dandy kayak gear storage bag and in front of it, a splash-proof boat box with rod holders bolted to it. Pretty cool! Below right: a crate cover, and below left, a splash-proof backpack.

This Tackle Webs bag snugs up beneath a frame seat on a Jackson Cuda. Note, too, the plier sheath.

Stick it Where the Sun Don't Shine

In Chapter 1, we emphasized the importance of finding a kayak and seat package that fits your body shape and provides the kind of support needed. Another consideration, if you're investing in a seat, is storage. Some models, such as the popular Surf to Summit series, may include zippered pouches in the back, drink holders and even rod holders. Frame seats, like those from Native, Jackson and Hobie, may also provide attachment points for various tackle- and tool-management systems.

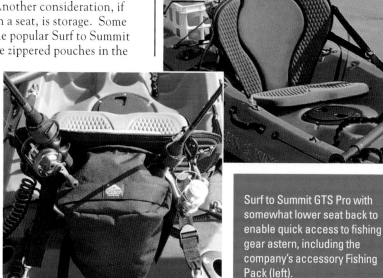

Surf to Summit GTS Pro with somewhat lower seat back to enable quick access to fishing gear astern, including the company's accessory Fishing Pack (left).

Lubricants and Rust Fighters

One of the wonders of kayak fishing is the simplified maintenance—no oil changes, no corroding engine components, no lower unit gear lube. At the same time, there are parts which demand attention. Medium-heavy aerosolized petroleum spray, such as Corrosion Stop, is useful for trailer components, exposed screws and other metallic surfaces. A lighter water-displacing spray, such as WD40, is handy for swivels, snap clips and other parts which you don't want to attract dust. The Penn Protect spray leaves a very fine mist on fishing reels and rod guide frames. The two products at bottom right are special reel lubes: The oil is for line rollers, ball bearings and handles; the lithium grease for gears and drive shafts. For pedal drives and specialized kayak components consult the manufacturer for the recommended lubricant.

Fish Bags

An insulated, zippered fish bag is a great thing to have, whether you're keeping fish or not. Fill it up with ice, or better yet, a mix of ice and some frozen water bottles. It'll double as a cooler for beverages.

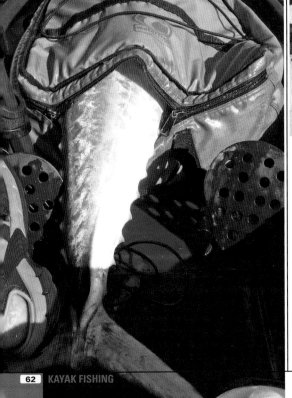

Rod leash for offshore adventures.

Leashes and Tethers

Kayakers are divided over the use of paddle leashes. Some feel they're essential insurance that if you capsize or drop your paddle, you aren't, well, up a creek without a paddle. Others, particularly some sea and whitewater kayakers, are wary of additional lines that you could become entangled in, or worse, choked.

The typical paddle leash has a velcro strap which wraps around the midpoint of the paddle shaft. The line itself is either a plastic spring-coil or a nylon-shrouded bungee. Some leashes have a snap (brass, bronze or stainless for saltwater) for attachment to an eyelet

Author adds camera holder using the Mighty Mount system for Yak Attack accessories.

on the kayak, while others have a nylon loop which may be hitched where desired.

As you might expect, these leashes can get in the way of your paddle stroke.

Similar leashes may be enlisted to help keep rods from falling over and sinking. These can be especially useful in choppy water, where you're paddling hard and focused on getting somewhere. Fishing rods have an uncanny habit of wiggling out of rod holders in these conditions.

Last but not least, two essential components which must have some form of leash or float strap: One, your pliers, and two, your camera. (I admit it—while researching this book, I dropped a pair of pliers into the Pacific Ocean off La Jolla, and a Canon D10—waterproof but not unsinkable—in Ding Darling Refuge in Florida.)

Retractable gear-keepers are great for pliers and other small tools, including lip grippers.

Camera Mounts

For starters, let's once and for all give up on the idea of taking self-portraits with catches held at arm's length or lying in our laps. It looks goofy—you're simply not going to look back years from now and say, "Wow! Look at that 18-inch redfish between my legs!" And of course, no one else wants to see those pictures, either.

Best thing on a kayak is a dedicated camera mount; you can build your own using PVC, twisty lamp grips, and other gear, but frankly for $50 or thereabouts, you're better off buying a commercially made system. Now you can position the camera to get a better perspective of your trophy catch—the color of the sky, the lure used, the expression on your face: These are the kinds of details that make for memorable shots.

Shown at right is the Panfish Portrait system from Virginia-based Yak Attack. It takes like 1

Yak Attack Panfish Portrait is adjustable, and the stem twists free when not needed.

You made a test snapshot to confirm where to put it, before drilling the holes, right?

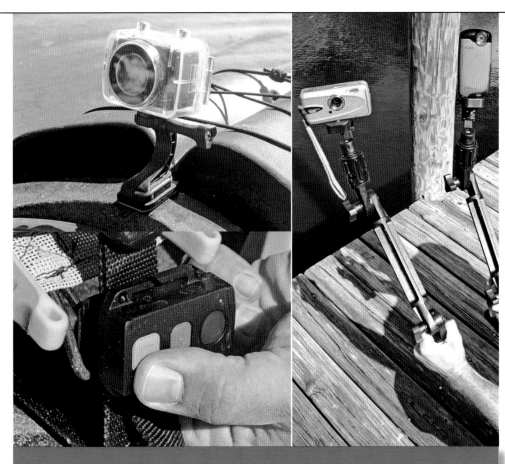

Lots of other systems are available for documenting your fishing trips. On the left is a remote-control camera. At right, a couple of extendable arms for the Scotty mounting system.

minute, 42 seconds to install. . . not counting the time you might spend goofing around figuring out the best place to put it (that's your author with a teddy bear—don't ask). Four stainless hex-head screws anchor the nylon Mighty-Mount base to the hull. A twist mechanism and T-bolt anchor the stem, and a RAM-style swivel ball mount can be adjusted to position the camera.

There's an interesting back-story to the Yak Attack system. The founder, Luther Cifers, is somewhat new to the kayak world. An industrial designer by trade, he lives in a central Virginia town called Farmville. And really likes Legos.

Luther Cifers paddled out on the York River, in Virginia, caught a croaker, then started a company!

"We used to do fall fishing trips to the Outer Banks, mostly the surf and piers," Luther told me in an interview. "One thing we liked was surf fishing for sharks. To get the baits out farther, my friend, Bob, bought a kayak. Years later, he started fishing out of it, then he started egging me on: 'You've gotta get a kayak!'"

In 2008, Luther paddled out on the York River, in Virginia, caught a croaker, then promptly started a kayak accessory company. By 2009, he had invented the Visi-Pole. Today, his company designs and builds all kinds of goodies, right there in Farmville, USA. How's that for home-grown!

Odds and Ends

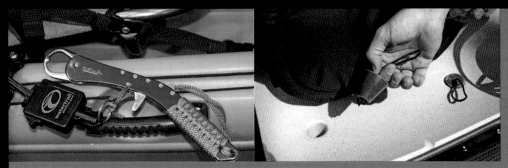

For fish grippers (left) and other tools, be sure to have a lanyard attached to the boat. Shown is a Water-trail retractable gear keeper. At right, scupper plugs are good to have; for long trips over relatively calm water, you can squish these down to keep water from splashing up below your seat.

Dry Boxes and Bags

There's a brisk market for watertight storage systems, and you can find boxes and soft bags to fit any kayak hatch. A true waterproof box will have a rubberized gasket and a locking lid.

Duct Tape

Always keep a roll in your truck or car. This stuff is a day-saver—or in the case of the author's Royalex canoe, a year-saver. The canoe shown here has been a backyard fixture at the author's home for more than 10 years. Beneath the duct tape patch is a hole as big as a deck of cards. It could be welded, but instead, the tape is replaced a few times a year. The hole has never leaked. Author figures he's spent $5 on 10 years worth of service (not counting spray paint for duck season). Gorilla Tape is said to be the best of all, for rotomolded polyethylene hulls.

Switching up Gear for Chesapeake Bay Region

Michael Guyer, a member of YakAttack's pro staff, compiled these informative photos demonstrating various applications for the company's GearTrac device systems. Retired from the Navy in 2000, Guyer lives in Suffolk, Virginia, where he works as a defense contractor.

"There is no such thing as a 'time of year' to fish the Chesapeake Bay," he says of his home waters. "We are the northernmost range for southern fishes and the southern-most migration for northern fishes. In the summer, we fish the salt for fish like cobia that have headed north and in the winter we chase the stripers that have headed south. I primarily use spinning gear for fishing the salt, with lures like plastics on jigheads being my go to, followed by topwaters. My favorites, particularly in the fall, are redfish, speckled trout and stripers. However, we have a great freshwater fishery here and I can be found chasing largemouth bass and crappie year-round, with a mix of baitcasting and spinning gear, particularly spinnerbaits, plastic frogs and the new turtle baits available."

From freshwater creeks to the Lynnhaven Inlet, below, Virginia kayakers call upon a wide range of gear.

Here a RAM rod holder is installed on a 12-inch piece of GearTrac. It may be moved forward or back using the Screwball base.

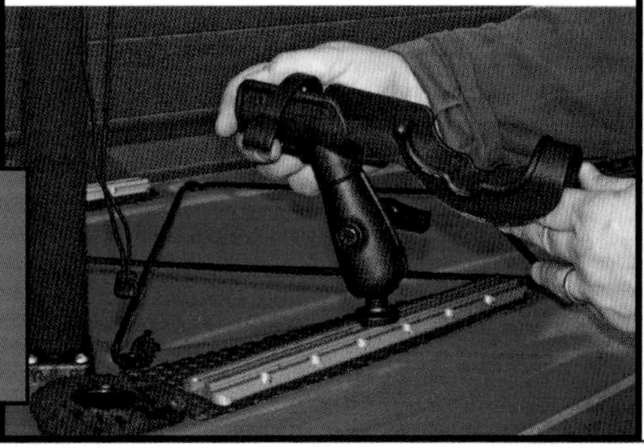

Shown here are a few applications for the Yak Attack GearTrac. Some kayak companies (Wilderness, for one) make their own track systems, or you might add one like this.

with lures like plastics on jigheads as go-to baits.

"My favorites are redfish and striped bass, and we have a great, year-round freshwater fishery for largemouth and crappie."

Michael Guyer, who contributed these photos, casts on Briery Creek, near Cumberland, VA.

Same GearTrac as last frame, but now a DogBone accessory has been substituted to hold a camera mount.

Impressive array of useful (and costly) electronics, easily removed or adjusted, depending upon the angler's goals for the day.

Fishfinder and GPS Plotters

Quick-release systems (Tallon, below) are available to move a combo sonar/GPS from one boat to another. Sweet setup!

Do you really need electronics on your kayak? If you're mostly fishing shallow coastal bays or ponds, probably not. Fishfinders are handy for finding subsurface structure and ledges, but in depths less than 10 feet, their utility for marking fish is questionable. A handheld GPS may be all you need to navigate your way around a tree-covered archipelago. For that matter, a compass, chart and basic understanding of navigation may be all you need to get you there and back.

But if finding deepwater structure, and marking and returning to precise waypoints, are part of your game, there are many options for mounting electronic devices on kayaks. Probably the best general setup, given limited deck space, is a combination fishfinder/GPS plotter. This allows you to select either feature, or use both in a split-screen mode (for this application, you'll be most satisfied with a color screen of at least 5 inches measured on diagonal). The GPS will likely have a built-in internal receiver which allows it to receive signals from the satellites orbiting the earth. All you need to do is supply power, in the form of a compact 12-volt battery or battery array in a water-resistant housing.

The fishfinder, or sonar, however, has an important accessory.

The working part of a fishfinder is the transducer, that smooth puck or rod which is attached to the main unit by a long cable. The transducer converts an electical impulse into a high-frequency sound wave. That sound wave travels down, and when it strikes an object, the wave returns. Because the speed of sound through water is constant, 4,800 feet per second, the processor can measure the time lapse between the signal transmission and the echo return to determine the distance. All this happens many times each second, resulting in a continuous wave on your fishfinder screen. Pass over a bunch of downed timber? You'll see the spiky outline on the screen, as the sonar waves return to the transducer at different intervals. Pass over a school of fish? You'll see their shapes in the form of arches.

Electronics manufacturers are quickly picking up on the needs of kayakers. Factory mounting kits are now available.

If you're installing a fishfinder on a kayak, there are many options, but it's important to note a few things.

One, you cannot cut and re-attach the transducer cable. These are precision cables to which the system is tuned. No, you don't need 20 feet of cable for your kayak, but in this case you'll have to find a way to deal with it. Stowing it belowdecks in loose coils works well; just don't bind the coils tightly.

Another thing to consider is the mounting of the transducer. A transducer is quite capable of sending and receiving signals through solid polyethylene or fiberglass. It will not, however, function properly if installed over a void in the material, or if there are air bubbles in the adhesive. Some kayakers mount the transducer in a flat spot in the hull, along the keel, for instance. In fiberglass powerboats, epoxy is often used to hold the transducer in place, but epoxy doesn't bind well to polyethylene. Lexel and Goop are two adhesives which may be used to secure a flexible, air- and water-tight bond.

Another option is a thru-scupper mount, which holds the transducer beneath the hull and carries the cable topside through a scupper. Lowrance and Humminbird both offer devices for this purpose. Or, you might build your own outboard transducer bracket using stainless fasteners and strips of Starboard or some other lightweight, waterproof material.

Electronics manufacturers are quickly picking up on the installation needs of kayakers, and there's a good chance you can buy a mounting kit from the factory. Alternately, RAM Mounts has a great variety of quick-disconnect and moveable mounting systems; these can be used to network with track products from Yak Attack and others. Tallon, a New Zealand firm, also sells many kinds of plug-and-play electronics mounts. The configurations are nearly endless.

Sport Fish for Kayakers

King Mackerel
(Scomberomorus cavalla)

◆**A.K.A.** Kingfish, King
◆**Range:** From Caribbean Sea north to Chesapeake region, and throughout Gulf of Mexico. Seasonal, favoring water temps above 70 degrees.
◆**Size:** 10 to 20 pounds fairly common. World record 93 pounds.
◆**Diet:** Menhaden, sardines and other schooling finfish.
◆**Kayak Tactics:** Trolling a lipped plug along the beach is a good way to hook kingfish. Also, catch live bait on the scene using a sabiki rig, then transfer to a fishing rod with a wire leader and small hook. Slow-troll or drift. Beware of sharp teeth.

Brian Nelli put a fishfinder to good use off Stuart, FL.

Guys have used all sorts of jerry-rigged bait containers. A flow-through plastic bucket, towed on a short nylon line, is fine for quick trips, where you aren't paddling far.

Hobie's ready-made livewell is a great setup: The pump draws water from one scupper, and the outflow passes through another scupper. This arrangement may be copied to

Factory Hobie

Homemade Tank

The two livewell systems shown, one from Hobie, the other built by California kayaker Andy Allen, are designed around the aft tank well, where the pump intake runs through a scupper hole.

Water from bottom drain of livewell runs out through the scupper hole on the opposite side. Make sure to use a round tank, so that baitfish may continue swimming without being trapped.

The Hobie model comes with its own battery. The home-built livewell will need a battery array in a waterproof box, such as this Pelican 1060. The wires pass through a rubber rigging grommet.

Cheap and indestructible, the plastic Flow Troll can house two dozen shrimp or about half that number of small baitfish.

suit other kayaks. Shown is a bucket customized for a Malibu kayak (the company also builds kayaks with center livewells—which cuts out twisting

around to fiddle with baits).

Like many aspects of kayak rigging, the options for livebait storage are limited only by your imagination.

The cockpit of this Malibu Stealth doubles as a casting platform and livewell.

Braided Line or Monofilament?

I n my ocean fishing trips, I almost always use monofilament, and then no more than 20-pound-test. With 20-pound mono, I've been towed (rapidly!) by 100-pound tarpon, giant jacks and other big fish. Line breakage was the least of my worries. Years ago, I fought a 27-pound jack crevalle for almost an hour on 8-pound-test IGFA-class monofilament. There were two of us in a 16-foot aluminum canoe, and the jack towed us around like we were barely there. The line held up, and I caught the fish.

All this begs the question of what kind of line do you really need.

The rage today is gelspun polyethylene, which is available in many configurations from a variety of line manufacturers. It's commonly referred to as braided line, though some products are thermally fused to form a single strand. (The polyethylene is similar to the material out of which rotomolded kayaks are made.) The stuff is very strong for its weight and diameter, and has little to no stretch. Bites are felt instantaneously, and hookset response is immediate. Casts go farther, in some cases.

Does that mean kayak fishermen should abandon nylon monofilament, or mono?

Not so fast.

There's a limit to how much pressure you can apply to a fish out of a kayak, and while we've yet to test it across the spectrum, it's pretty clear that a fisherman aboard a movable vessel, not permanently moored, will have a difficult time breaking 30- or 50-pound braided line. It's difficult to do that from a powerboat at anchor or even under engine power! Even 8-pound test is extremely hard to break, assuming you've tied good knots and aren't fighting a fish around abrasive structure. So the appeal of very-high breaking strength is lost somewhat.

One place braid does excel over mono, for kayakers anyway, is in providing immediate, clear connection to bottom fishing lures and baits. Because the kayak is subject to wave action and current, it's helpful to have a straight connection to the hook, with as little scope as possible.

The same reasoning applies for very light plastic lures, with which monofilament may be subject to wind and current.

At left, ocean-class spinning outfit with 20-pound-test monofilament; middle, long-cast spinner with 10-pound braid for flats; at right, low-profile baitcaster with 12-pound-test mono, for topwaters and crankbaits.

It's very important to consider where you'll be fishing, and to what extent you might face risks of capsizing or entanglement. Braided line can produce very bad cuts if a fish suddenly runs off while you're untangling things. If you happen to get tied up with a big tarpon or wrapped in your line after falling in the surf, the thought of getting 30-pound braid around your neck is terrifying indeed.

Which is why I normally fish monofilament in tricky situations, and always have a safety knife handy. I use a cheap dive knife in an ankle sheath; the point has been ground away, as there's no need to stab anything.

I like to use braided polyethylene line when I'm on the flats, usually the 10- or 15-pound class. If I'm casting topwaters or other hard baits with treble hooks (usually only when wading), then I'll use monofilament in the same weight class. I like a little stretch with hard baits, to reduce the likelihood of fish throwing the hooks.

Regardless of your line choice, resist the urge to jerk or buggy-whip the rod to pull a lure out of a shoreline snag. That lure or sinker might come at you like a rifle bullet, and in the kayak there's little space to dodge such a projectile. Better to go clear it yourself. SB

CHAPTER 5

Safety and Rescue

Can you handle turbulent waves, currents and winds? Do you know how to recover after capsizing? Shallow water conditions vary dramatically from overhead waters. Know exactly what to do when that "Oh no!" situation occurs.

With kayak fishermen headed for the horizon regularly, safety is more important than ever. Fishing with a buddy goes a long way, too. All kayakers should prepare a float plan with family or friends before launching.

Don't forget to cover your bases when on the water. Personal flotation devices, lanyards, lights, flags, and floats are just some of the vital tools you should have accessible in the cockpit. For electronics, a VHF radio may be your only form of communication if out of cellphone range.

Let's get started.

For safety's sake, be prepared with the proper tools, electronics and accessories when on the water. You never know when you're going to need it.

Two kayakers head off-shore on the east coast of Florida. Boaters facing into the sun may have a hard time seeing them.

Stay Afloat

The U.S. Coast Guard requires you to have two safety items on a kayak: An approved personal flotation device (PFD) and a whistle or other sound-producing device. If you venture out after dark, you must also have a means of signalling visually, a waterproof flashlight, for instance.

That's just the beginning of a safety plan.

Designed for kayakers: Astral Buoyancy V-Eight Type III vest, with mesh and reflective accents.

That PFD? Wear it. If you doubt that advice, try putting on a PFD while you're in the water. And then try to do it in moving water, after your kayak and all your gear has been dumped by a wave. About the only exception would be ankle-deep water in the subtropics, in midsummer heat, where you're merely using the kayak to skim your way to a redfish flat. (Some pictures in other chapters of this book, I confess, illustrate Florida anglers preserving thermal comfort while apparently dismissing personal safety. I vouch that the water was less than 2 feet deep, but still.)

High-back kayaking PFDs may be more comfortable than traditional powerboat vests—they are designed to ride above the seatback, keeping your lower back in alignment. However, in order to provide the requisite amount of flotation, the kayak PFDs move more foam to the front, which can make them feel somewhat bulky, at first.

Ed Stout showed some new designs from Astral Buoyancy, an accessory company based in Asheville, N.C. The vests have air holes to allow them to breathe.

High-visibility colors are smart, and if the vest is not already equipped with reflective tape or piping, you might add some of your own. It's also easy to add reflective tape to the kayak itself.

A whistle is a sensible addition to a kayak PFD. A VHF or cell phone is of some utility in dire straights, but in a worst-case scenario, that shrill whistle requires only your breath; besides that, it makes a good alert signal for non-emergency situations— two blasts for, let's go home, or whatever signal you and your buddies agree on. (Ten blasts for, "Come take a picture of this big fish, why don't you!") Signal flares may be a lifesaver, if you're far from shore.

Having a required PFD and distress whistle is just the beginning of a safety plan.

An inflatable paddle float is handy for re-entering the kayak after a spill: You slide it over one blade of the paddle, pump it up, and use it to stabilize the boat while you climb back aboard. Wedge the other end of the paddle under a bungee.

A high-visibility floating throw rope is also good to carry. This is a whitewater kayaking necessity, but it's also valuable on flat water trips: If your paddling partner gets into trouble, you may need to tow him or her back to the landing.

A short paddle blade, stowed belowdecks, may save the day if you or a buddy lose your main paddle. Davis Instruments, a supplier of marine accessories, makes a 20-inch telescoping paddle that extends to 40 inches.

In tropical climates, "Palm Beach Pete" Hinck wears an inflatable suspender-type PFD.

Throw Ropes and Paddle Floats

Throw-bag with floating polypropylene rescue line is standard gear on whitewater trips, and handy in the sea, too.

Tom Reilly, a sea kayak instructor from Central California, simulates climbing back into the kayak, using the paddle as a stabilizer.

Paddle float (this one's made by GAIA) slips over the blade and inflates.

The paddle may now be used to assist in retaking the kayak. (Tom is a very good sport.)

VHF Radio

We're hooked on cellular phones these days, but for emergency communications in the marine environment, VHF (Very High Frequency) radios are superior.

Even at introductory prices in the $90 range, you'll find handheld, rechargeable VHF radios built to solid specifications, far more durable than a cell phone. Full-featured, waterproof units cost slightly more. Floating models are available, too, a sensible investment for the kayak angler contemplating rescue situations.

These devices work on ship-to-ship or ship-to-station radio transmission—service coverage is free and mostly uniform around the country. No fiddling around with a tiny keypad to dial a phone number. You press a button, anyone within range hears you.

In the case of handheld VHF, as long as you're within 5 or 6 miles of another VHF radio, or as much as 12 miles from a land-based Coast Guard station, you should be able to get help. Fixed-mount, 25-watt units with accessory antennas will transmit farther, but installing this type of system on a kayak is going a bit too far—literally and figuratively.

The Coast Guard and many local

Floating models are a sensible investment for the kayaker.

emergency service providers—including fish and wildlife officers—monitor VHF Channel 16 at all times. So do private and commercial vessels, and so should you, if you have a VHF radio on board.

Do note that losing a paddle does not constitute a "mayday" event. Nor does drifting into open water while struggling to paddle into the wind. In cases like this, you'd announce your identity and your situation—in that order—on Channel 16 by pressing and holding the transmit button and beginning with the two words "Pan-pan," sounding like "Pawn-pawn," pronounced three times in series. This tells everyone to "Listen close, this is serious ... but I'm not in a life-threatening situation." Or, simply call "U.S. Coast Guard, U.S. Coast Guard, this is Oceak Kayak Blue, over."

Then release the transmit button and listen for instructions.

If you're stranded on a sandbar, inconvenienced but otherwise in no danger, odds are you'll be connected with a local tow service (be prepared to pay). Or, perhaps a nearby boater may volunteer to pick you up.

Some examples of genuine mayday distress: experiencing signs of a heart attack; actually sinking your vessel; drifting out to sea in that strong wind after losing your paddle—and after having exhausted other means of communication. A "Mayday, mayday,

A handheld VHF radio is a good thing to have. So is a well-equipped buddy.

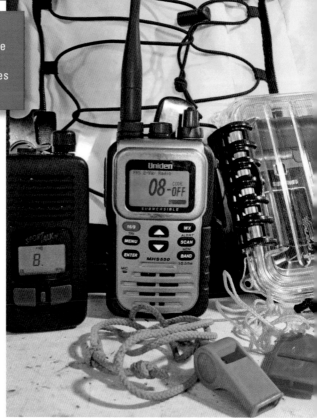

mayday" announcement on VHF 16 tells authorities to begin mobilizing an array of search and rescue vessels. Listen closely to instructions, and be prepared to give as much information as possible about your location and circumstances.

The Standard Horizon HX851 pictured on page 78 ($249) is among the industry's best-equipped handhelds. It has transmission power to 6 watts, meets the floating/waterproof criteria, and offers a GPS-equipped Digital Selective Calling (DSC) mode: Meaning you can press the Distress key and issue a distress signal that includes your latitude and longitude, as well as your Maritime Mobile Service Identity, or MMSI.

The MMSI logs important details about your vessel in the Coast Guard's national distress database: your name, radio type, emergency contacts ashore, vessel description, and more. You must register to receive an MMSI (www.boatus.com); when you do so, you'll see a space for "vessel registration or documentation." If your DSC-enabled handheld will be used on an unregistered kayak or canoe, simply write in "see remarks." In the remarks section, indicate what vessels the VHF will be used on: Ocean Kayak Trident 13, yellow.

Multiband VHF and FRS

Want to keep in touch with a couple of buddies spread out around the lake? Maybe listen to FM radio while you're fishing? A combination VHF radio, usually known as a multiband radio, is a sweet setup. Author's Uniden MHS550 submersible VHF has the option of tuning to Family Radio Service (FRS) channels, allowing the unit to communicate instantly with inexpensive "walkie-talkies." Only downside is this radio doesn't float if dropped, but that's easy to remedy with a floating wrist lanyard.

In a busy marine environment, where safety and commerce are at stake, it's not polite to clog up VHF channels with chit-chat. Hailing another vessel on VHF 16, and then moving to an approved channel, is acceptable, if you have an important vessel-to-vessel message relating to navigation: "Ocean Kayak Blue, Ocean Kayak Blue, Ocean Kayak Blue, this is Malibu Green..."

"Malibu Green, this is Ocean Kayak Blue, over."

"Ocean Kayak Blue, switch to 71, over."

Now on 71, or some other approved channel: "See that storm on the horizon?" or "I'm heading back to the landing."

But for little things like, "Hey, they're biting on chartreuse ... what are you doing?" or "There's a school of reds coming your way!", that's what FRS channels are tailor-made for. Walkie-talkies are super cheap—for $20 a pair, you can loan one to a buddy and never have to shout over the flats again.

As a plus, most multiband VHF radios can tune into NOAA weather service frequencies, as well as FM or AM radio. The author, in fact, starts his day with a weather report on the handheld, then enjoys listening to the morning news during a sunrise, pre-work paddle.

Think Like a Powerboater

Bright vest, bright paddle blade, bright flag: This kayaker wants to be seen. You should, too.

Think like a powerboater. Such is good advice for the aspiring kayak fisherman. The point is, put yourself in the position of a person at the helm of a large boat. Perhaps that person is a new boater, or possibly suffering some impairment of judgment. Maybe there's an autopilot turn on, and the skipper is talking about the day's events with his friends. I bring this up not to cast aspersions on powerboaters, but rather to elucidate an important safety consideration, perhaps the most important one of all. You can lift yourself back onto a kayak after falling off. You can swim out of the breakers. You can wrap a bandage on a minor wound.

You don't come back from a collision with a high-speed powerboat. There's likely to be no second chance, no opportunity for you to inform the world that you, the kayaker, were in the right, and he, the powerboater, was running outside a channel, or not giving proper lookout.

The point of this is, because of the kayak's small footprint and relative difficulty of maneuvering to avoid danger, it's vital that you, the paddler,

VISICarbon Pro light folds up and stows in its own flag, when not in use.

protect yourself. Do not assume a powerboat can see you. Take what precautions you can—wearing a bright PFD, swinging bright paddle blades, a source of light at dawn and dusk. Attach an orange flag to a fishing rod or light pole. Ultimately, however, it's in your best interest to avoid busy channels, and never put yourself in a position where a vessel is bearing down on you. Don't let your life hinge on a guess that the skipper sees you and is prepared to steer away.

One common problem occurs near ocean inlets in the early morning and late afternoon. A pow-

Snook see in the dark just fine. Can't say the same for powerboaters. Even a homemade light is a good precaution.

erboater heading into a rising (or setting) sun has very limited sight, and might easily miss a kayak. I've seen this myself from the helm several times along the lower Florida Atlantic coast.

A sensible rule of thumb, if you must use an inlet, is to immediately paddle to the outside of a roughly 90-degree triangle extending directly from the inlet to sea. The object is not only to avoid the busiest routes in and out of the inlet, but also to move yourself out of the silhouette and into clear light. Far better, really, to use a calm beach launch far from the popular inlet; the fishing's likely better there anyway.

Kayaks and other paddle-powered vessels are not obligated to show navigation or white lights under Coast Guard regulations—only to have at

hand some means of illuminating, a flashlight, for instance. However, it makes very good sense to place a white all-round light on your kayak in the low-light periods. Pole lights are handy.

The Yak Attack light has a white LED that runs off AA batteries. A collapsible model is especially handy, as you can fold it up and stow it in a hatch after the sun rises.

Some kayakers are tempted to show red and green navigation lights, but my own feeling is, it's better not to. The red (port) and green (starboard) lights are designed to inform other vessels of your course; see a red light with a white light above, and you know the boat is passing to your port side. See both red and green lights, and that white light directly over them, and you know the vessel is bearing down on you, and you must take evasive action. Now: See only a white light, and as a powerboater (and paddler), you may infer two things: One, the boat is running away from you, or two, the boat is anchored.

Here's how it might work with a kayak. If the operator of a powerboat sees your red light and white light, he or she might assume you are making headway perpendicular to his course. As the "stand down" vessel (always yield to starboard, or right, just like arriving at a four-way intersection in a car), the boater will either slow down, or steer to starboard, planning to pass behind your course.

What you really want to show the powerboater is (and remember the foregoing discussion on avoiding these scenarios in the first place), you are not moving. You are to be avoided.

Again, show the white light, red and green, too, if it makes you more comfortable. But in the final analysis, don't fool around with fate. Night kayaking on a quiet lake or backwater can be exciting and relatively safe, but stay away from primary powerboating areas.

Never trust your life to another mariner's ability to recognize and interpret your signals.

Know Your Limits

The foregoing discussion opens up important questions all kayakers must address. Am I truly qualified, and equipped, to handle these waters? Is my vessel appropriate for the circumstances, and the range?

In assessing these issues, don't focus on what you can do in ideal conditions, but instead focus on the what-ifs. Sure, you're strong and capable of paddling 2 miles offshore. But what will you do if a storm arises? What if you run out of drinking water? What if you become tired paddling into the tide? The Coast Guard has an amazing array of vehicles and well-trained, courageous personnel ready to intervene in dire situations, but if anything, awareness of what's at stake should deter you from putting yourself in harm's way.

It's prudent seamanship to always think first of the other men and women on the water—the ones who may truly need life-saving resources. Your ill-conceived kayak adventure into heavy water might not only place unnecessary burden on taxpayers, but cost someone their life.

Don't regard a handheld VHF as a free ride home. Ditto for a Personal Locator Beacon, or PLB: These powerful, diminutive devices are a wise investment as a last-line of help in remote waters. When you press the distress button, sending your identity code, latitude and longitude to a satellite relay system, a huge network of rescue services rolls into motion.

In preparing for a trip, the first question shouldn't be, how are we going to get there, but rather, how are we going to return.

If only all days started and ended this calm, and fishy.

SafetyTips
for Moving Water

Special thanks to James McBeath, Director, World Kayak Initiative

•If whitewater is going to be your playground, go for lessons. You must learn to assess the risks and understand techniques for self-rescue and rescue of others.

•Never paddle alone.

•Learn to make strong, aggressive paddlestrokes for maneuvering in and out of moving water. Learn to use your torso, not just your arms to paddle.

•Dress appropriately for the conditions and season. The number one killer in moving water isn't actually current, it's the cold.

•Have the general safety and rescue gear: PFD, whistle, throwbag with rope, and helmet if the run is rocky.

•Recognize the levels of whitewater, Class 1 to V, and know where your personal kayaking skills can take you.

•Ensure you have the proper style boat, outfitted for the conditions.

•Never stand up in shallow moving water. Foot entrapment (between boulders, for example) is the number one cause of drowning; even in a foot or two of water, you can be knocked over and held down.

•Scout each rapid you don't know. Whenever in doubt, carry (portage) your kayak around questionable areas.

•Look for, and avoid, branches, log-jams or other objects that can entrap you and your boat (strainers).

•Look for, and avoid, holes (hydraulics) or low-head dams that can trap you and your boat.

•Look for escape routes in case of a swim.

•Set up safety spotter if needed.

•Always tilt boat downstream when entering a current or upstream edge will get caught.

•Self rescue: Learn whitewater techniques for rolling and escape. If you fall out, try to keep with boat, but let it go if it is bringing you to an even more dangerous spot. Try to hold onto your paddle. Swim with feet up, pointing downstream to bounce off rocks.

•Learn team rescue tactics, as well as CPR and first aid for hypothermia.

•Never anchor in moving water.

Sport Fish for Kayakers

Red Drum (Sciaenops ocellatus)

◆**A.K.A.** Redfish, Channel Bass, Reds

◆**Range:** Western Atlantic and Gulf of Mexico waters from Long Island, NY, through southern Texas. Tolerates water temps from upper 40s to low 90s.

◆**Size:** Inshore specimens typically 16 to 27 inches. Adult drum to 50 pounds thrive in open waters along the coastline. World record 94 pounds, 2 ounces.

◆**Diet:** Crabs, shrimp, finfish.

◆**Kayak Tactics:** Look for tails or wakes in shallow water as reds feed nose-down over seagrass or oysters. Wade, paddle or toe-creep into position and cast soft-plastic bait or live shrimp. In deeper water, stake or anchor near channel where safe to do so, and soak crab or live pinfish on bottom.

Thad Day pulls in this nice South Florida redfish.

Sit-on-Top Recovery

1

Something we all have to practice. Do it in the deep end. First, reach under the kayak and grab the opposite side.

2

Pull down on the opposite side and push up on the near side to judo-flip the kayak into an upright position.

3

Secure your paddle so it doesn't drift away. Catch your breath so you don't, either.

4

Kick and hoist your carcass into the kayak.

5

Okay, you're on your belly. Now flip over and pull your knee around so that you're seated.

6

All right! Now how about we stock some fish in this swimming pool . . .

A Few Words on Weather and Currents

Environmental hazards specific to various kinds of fishing will be addressed in later chapters. But regardless of where and when you launch, be mindful of wind and current. Arrive at a backwater launch and you may find tidal current barely perceptible. However, a quarter-mile away, at a constriction between islands, the tide may be rushing like a river.

Time your trip accordingly. In a semi-diurnal tide region (the U.S. Atlantic coast, for instance) you might paddle out during the last few hours of outgoing tide, then catch the incoming tide on the way in. In mixed-tide regions, such as the Central Florida Gulf Coast, be aware that tides may "stand" for a few hours on certain days of the month; that means an outgoing tide may cease flowing, only to resume and possibly accelerate. Ignore the pattern and you could find yourself struggling to make headway—and if you've been injured or otherwise compromised, more than personal comfort may be at stake.

A good rule for wind is, always paddle into the wind. Sea kayakers in Southern California obey this rule diligently; some days, unexpected

> **Never paddle with the wind without reckoning the effort needed for the return trip.**

and sustained bursts of wind come down off the mountains and really hinder return trips to the beach. If the wind suddenly piles on, the guys paddle for the beach, no questions asked.

On a lake or bay, never paddle across with the wind without reckoning the effort required for the return trip.

Deal with thunderstorms and big cold fronts by avoiding them! In Florida, most every summer day begins with clear blue skies and light winds, and nearly every afternoon ends with a wicked thunderstorm. We plan our fishing trips early to avoid the weather. Most days I'm off the water by 10 a.m. When the storm subsides, there may be a window of calm in the evening that affords some fishing time. Learn the patterns for your area.

Lost your kayak? An ID decal from the Coast Guard auxiliary may not only help you get your boat back, but alert rescuers to your status. U.S. Coast Guard Alaska actually rescued a stranded girl after a fishing vessel found her unattended, but identifiable, kayak.

Vessel Identification Sticker for Canoe, Kayak or Rowboat

IF FOUND - CONTACT

Name: Jeff Weakley

Phone:

Phone:

Use waterproof marker

Dealing With Hooks

There's no way around it. If you're a kayak fisherman, you're going to be dealing with hooks. Single hooks are best, for the simple reason that they're easier to remove from fish without jabbing yourself in the process. But some lures simply perform better with trebles. You can make a few modifications to make things safer, as explained here. Sooner or later, though, you'll end up with a hook in your body. You'll be much happier if it's a barbless one.

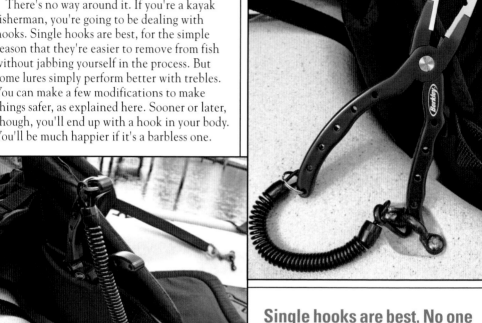

Single hooks are best. No one wants to remove a treble hook from skin when the waves are rocking and rolling.

You'll want pliers to dehook your catches, but have you thought about de-barbing your hooks? It's a very good idea. Simply press the barb flat.

This is the author's pick gaff. It can be used to de-hook large fish, as shown below right.

The author's gaff, built from a 12/0 hook, serves as a de-hooker or fish-sticker. Cover the hook with a pool noodle when not in use.

More Tools for Trouble

A dive knife or sharp blade that's well-protected and immediately accessible is a vital tool for kayak anglers. You might one day need it to free yourself from fishing line or some other entanglement. Shown below is a fancy titanium model from NRS, with an attachment system for your paddling vest. This one has a bottle-opener for you to use while retelling your harrowing story of escape.

A manual bilge pump, or bailer, is another one of those tools that you rarely use, but one day might. This model is lightweight and stows easily in a kayak. It can be used to remove water from inside hulls or hatches. A device like this is a must-have for a sit-inside or hybrid kayak, and a should-have, for at least one of your party of sit-on-top anglers. They're inexpensive, at $20 to $30.

When the situation arises, a manual bilge pump, right, or dive knife, below, is vital.

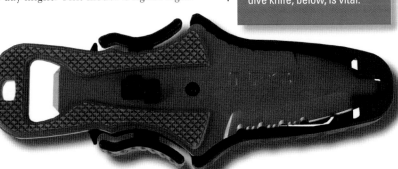

CHAPTER 6

Comfort

At the end of the day, there's no prize given for endurance. A big fish may be rewarded, possibly, if you're in a tournament. But for most of us, we're greeted by obligations of home, family or work. Keeping oneself comfortable and preserving some measure of energy is therefore a worthy endeavour for the kayak angler.

There's also personal safety to consider. Are you dressed properly for the environment? What happens if you or a buddy fall into the water? If you're planning to wade-fish, do you have protective footwear? Before we head out to fish, let's look at some of the options.

Keeping yourself comfortable and preserving some measure of energy is a worthy endeavour. Let's look at some of the options.

Get back, Jack: You had a great day, even kept the sun off your face. But will you have energy left for home or work?

Our Wet World

Let's start with basic attire. Fact: You don't have to soak your butt all day in cold water to be a real kayak fisherman. We've already discussed alternative seating modes for hybrid kayaks and sit-on-tops, where the seat may be raised above water level, but regardless of seat elevation, it's wise to invest in a pair of waterproof, breathable waders or paddling pants. In very cold seasons, the benefits extend to thermal protection. And waders are

Mesh sandals, above, are nice for tropical climes. Below is a sample of the author's many boating and wading shoes.

Keep your butt dry with paddling pants, like these Immersion Research Comp Pants. Neoprene waistband and neoprene ankle gaskets help seal out the elements. These pants are constructed using a minimal amount of seams, out of 4-layer waterproof/breathable material (same used in dry suits). Sizes range from Small to XX Large. Lots of options to choose from on the market.

great, especially if you plan to do any wade-fishing. Chest-waders are usually the best choice if the day will entail serious wading, while pant-length models are preferred if most of the fishing will be done aboard the kayak.

Appropriate fit is important, and you'll want some form of wicking base layer beneath the pants, as direct contact of skin on GoreTex and other membrane-fabrics is rather uncomfortable. Thin wool or synthetic long underwear are good choices.

In warm weather, or for short trips, you can do without the waterproof pants, instead wearing a pair of lightweight, quick-drying nylon or polyester pants. Surf shorts are another good summer alternative. Just don't wear jeans and cotton underwear.

Always expect to get wet—whether from waves washing over the boat, drip from the paddle, or even a brief rain shower. Either wear something that repels water, or dries out quickly. Same goes for tops.

Footwear is another topic. Zippered neoprene wading booties are highly commendable, either as a sensible, protective terminus for bare-legged summer adventures, or covering the stocking feet of waders (much better than heavy boot-foot waders, and ultimately safer in the event of a capsize).

Quick-drying tennis-shoe style boating shoes are another option, and better than neoprene boots if you must walk a long way to launch. Sandals have come a long way, too, in terms of

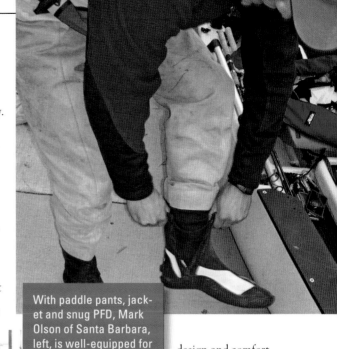

With paddle pants, jacket and snug PFD, Mark Olson of Santa Barbara, left, is well-equipped for the cool Cali coast. Top: neoprene booties over breathable stocking-foot waders.

design and comfort.

Reconsider the temptation to fish barefoot. You might launch from a friendly, sandy stretch of beach, only to find the need to step out of the boat into unfamiliar waters, where oyster bars or other sharp terrain await.

Another mark in favor of closed-toe footwear: Protecting your feet from fishhooks and the fish themselves. In my early ocean kayaking forays, I quickly tipped the balance away from barefeet after hauling a few kingfish into the boat. It seems great to feel the breeze on your toes, but nothing ruins a day quicker than a treble hook or a mackerel incisor in your foot—or both.

In cold weather, a waterproof breathable paddling jacket is a good addition—again under the assumption that you will get wet, even under a bluebird sky. In any weather, some form of rain jacket is valuable, stuffed into a gear bag where you may retrieve it as needed.

You'll meet him in a later chapter, but for now, a masked Greg Timmer brings you a message: Avoid the Florida sun.

The familiar combination of hat and polarized sunglasses warrants at least a short mention. The benefits for the sight-fisherman are obvious: The sunglasses cut off glare and allow you to see beneath the surface; the hat, too, reduces distracting overhead light and helps your eyes adjust to interpret details in the darker water. Health benefits are also apparent. In a kayak, with no top, you're subject to a barrage of UV rays. The full scalp protection of a hat, instead of a visor, is sensible. And a wide brim to limit exposure to your neck and ears is also a good idea. On that score, a soft Buff or balaclava-style face-and-neck covering may be added. The skin around your shirt collar is especially vulnerable to UV exposure while paddling.

Gloves, too, are available to minimize UV exposure.

Give heed to hydration and nourishment, before, during and after fishing. In hot weather, bring what you think you'll need to drink—and then double it in the form of frozen water bottles stashed in your cooler, fish bag, or an available hatch. Not only can the frozen bottles be enlisted to keep your lunch or your catch cool, they'll provide a long-term supply of cool water in the event of an emergency.

Energy bars are good to have on board, but for all-day trips nothing beats a sandwich pulled out of a portable cooler. Beginning the day on a full stomach, it often seems acceptable to launch with little in the way of food, but that's your fish-brain tricking you. By the afternoon, you'll find that fasting leads to fatigue, which not only makes paddling and fishing more burdensome, but likely means you're shot for the rest of the day. With family or friends anticipating your happy, smiling face, instead there you are again, shuffling zombie-like into the pantry, stuffing your face with starchy junk food, ambling afterward toward an irretrievable slumber on the couch.

And if you ignored everything else in this chapter, you might well be scratching your butt and hunting around for peroxide to treat the cuts in your feet. Or worse, being treated for hypothermia or skin cancer.

A portable cooler with nutritious, energy-rich food is great to have.

One of the author's most prized possessions: An inexpensive Peet shoe dryer. This one's been in the garage for 15 years and works as well as the day it came out of the box. Radiant heating coils circulate warm air through shoes or boots. Soaking-wet boat shoes will dry overnight, extending shoe life for years. Also cuts back on stinky bacteria growth.

Author's boots for wading in oyster country. Yes, they're shredded up, but think of how the feet inside would've fared.

Know How to Handle Your Targeted Fish

Know the fish you're targeting! There's simply not enough room in a kayak for you and a spiky or toothy fish whose behavior and anatomy is unfamiliar to you. Nets and lip grippers are good tools for safely restraining a fish for dehooking or measuring, but nothing beats studying up on what kinds of fish you'll expect to catch, and how local anglers handle them.

Some fish, such as largemouth bass, come with their own hand-holds—in the case of bass, a sturdy, raspy and altogether harmless lower jaw. You can slide your thumb into the bass's mouth, grip the jaw and hold the fish while removing the hook. Try that with a bluefish, and the first thing to be removed will be a sizable chunk of your flesh! Here's a few tips on grips, so to speak:

Jack crevalle

You're going to catch bunches of these in coastal waters. Small ones you can immobilize by gripping over the shoulders and squeezing the black spot. Mark Naumovitz (art director for this book) brought out a lip-gripper for this large jack.

Snook

The lip grip works fine, just as with bass. Support the belly of big ones (over 6 pounds or so). Do not grab the gill plate, or attempt an over-the-shoulder grip, as you might with the crevalle. Snook have incredibly sharp, serrated blades hidden on the outside of their gill plates. They can cause severe lacerations.

Trout

Two good ways to handle seatrout. One is with a nylon or metal lip-gripper, without hoisting the fish out of the water. Second-best is with a very soft, knotless, fine-mesh landing net that cradles the fish without tearing the fins. If no device is available, wet your hands and grab the fish over the thick part of the shoulder. Or, use a glove and grip the lower jaw; just don't stick a bare finger in there—those teeth are sharp!

Sharks

Best not to fool with sharks in a kayak. But if you do, use a single, light-wire, non-stainless steel hook and pinch the barb down. You may be able to remove the hook with a short gaff, catching the bend of the hook and pulling it free. Otherwise, cut the leader close and the fish will eventually reject or dissolve the hook.

Flounder

Net them! Otherwise they're apt to shake loose next to the boat. No real good place for fingers or hands on these toothy, slippery flatfish. Gary Naumovitz, left, does show one way to pose a flounder. If not careful though, dinner will be slipping through your fingers.

Know How to Handle Your Targeted Fish

Ladyfish
Biggest worry is not the mouth but the other end.
Point them away from you or risk being sprayed.

Catfish

All kinds: Most catfish have sharp, stiff spines at the foremost edge of the dorsal (back) and pectoral (side) fins. A catfish flipper, or dehooker, is a good way to shake off the small ones. Shown below is a metal gripper for safely cradling a catfish; the plastic lid we added to highlight the spine. Big freshwater cats may be grabbed by the lower jaw. In a kayak it's probably best not to handle catfish at all. Definitely don't fool around with saltwater cats: Their spines (note serrations in the photos) cause excruciating pain. Drop one in your lap, your day is finished.

Saltwater catfish spines cause excruciating pain. Drop one in your lap, and you're finished.

Hypothermia

Comfort isn't the only consideration, when you're dressing for a kayak fishing trip. Also be prepared for the what-ifs: What happens if someone capsizes, or you miscalculate weather or currents?

Victims of mild hypothermia, shivering but capable of rational conversation, may need only warm, dry clothes and perhaps a nonalcoholic sip from a Thermos to recover. If a victim becomes confused or nonresponsive, you'll need to take immediate steps to evacuate that person for proper first aid. Communicate with emergency personnel using a VHF or cellular phone. Severe hypothermia definitely counts as a distress call. Until help arrives, focus on rewarming the victim's core with dry blankets, perhaps your own body heat in a huddle. Do not massage or apply warm compresses to the victim's arms or legs. SB

A collapsible dry bag like this one from NRS is perfect for stowing a spare fleece and a blanket. They could help save a life if someone takes a plunge far from port.

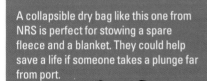

Sport Fish for Kayakers

Chinook Salmon
(Oncorhynchus tshawytscha)

◆**A.K.A.** King Salmon, Tyee

◆**Range:** Pacific Coast from northern California to Alaska. Hatchery-reared populations inhabit Great Lakes.

◆**Size:** 10 to 20 pounds. World record 97 pounds, 4 ounces

◆**Diet:** Small schooling fish, such as sardines, alewifes

◆**Kayak Tactics:** Timing essential, as open-water chinooks may be hundreds, if not thousands, of miles from shore! When adults approach Pacific rivermouths in early summer (late summer for Great Lakes), troll lipped diving plugs or spoons.

Joe Kaftan, who we met in Chapter 2, displays a nice chinook salmon.

CHAPTER 7

Hauling Your Kayak

Store your kayak indoors, if possible, or at least in a shaded area out of the sun. Protecting the hull from UV rays will extend its life. There are racks on the market for cradling a kayak without distorting its shape, but many owners simply build their own, using PVC pipe, cheap lumber or flat nylon straps and secure hangers.

When you're ready to head for the water, there are many options for carrying a kayak on a car or truck. The important thing is to choose a system that ensures your kayak remains safely attached while en route. Also consider the weight of the vessel, or vessels, and whether you'll feel comfortable lifting it overhead. Roof rack systems are versatile and compact, but many kayakers eventually invest in a trailer or full-size truck.

Choose a system that ensures your kayak remains safely attached. Also, will you be comfortable lifting the kayak overhead? Or will you prefer a trailer?

Fun in the Florida sun: Owner of the kayak above "hitched" a ride on the accompanying outboard skiff. At home, hide your kayak from the sun, and support the hull. Shown below is a homemade PVC rack on wheels, and at right, a wooden rack.

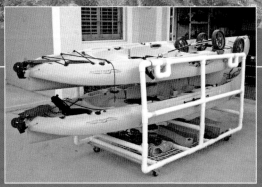

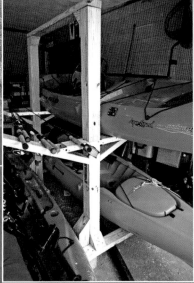

Trailers

Beautiful, multi-functional aluminum-frame trailer built by a Florida fabrication shop.

At one end of the spectrum, you can buy an inflatable kayak that comes in a stuff sack light enough to tote on a bicycle.

At the other end, you might want a fully loaded, pedal-powered, rotomolded kayak that scales 150 pounds.

As simple as kayaks are, transporting them leads to some inescapable realities. For anglers familiar with the powerboat lifestyle, the ghost of trailers past might rear its rusty head. Yes, you've escaped engine maintenance, but in some ways you're back where you started: Rinsing off trailers, checking bearing grease, replacing tires, constantly re-rigging trailer lights.

Wait a second, can't I just load that thing on top of the car? Well, yes and no.

If you're routinely hauling two or more kayaks whose combined weight exceeds 200 pounds, you should consider investing in a trailer. You may find the ease of loading and unloading justifies the expense.

Many trailer companies produce well-balanced rigs especially designed for kayaks and other small boats. The Trailex SUT (Small Utility Trailer) series is a good kayak-hauler, with the potential to carry as many as four vessels, depending on the model. The Dooit system, from Activity Trailer, is another one; you buy the base trailer and add on factory T-bars, as well as Thule or Yakima accessories. Both trailers will come in around $1,200.

On a trailer the kayak is not quite as exposed to windage as on a roof rack, but nonetheless you should lash the kayaks securely using proper nylon straps with locking mechanisms.

One wrinkle, if you go the trailer route: You will need to consult your state department of motor vehicles for titling and registration requirements.

A 250-series Trailex trailer, above, easily carries two heavyweight kayaks. The anglers below bought an old trailer from a rental service in need of cash.

And odds are you'll have to make an appearance at the local tax collector's office. In Florida, for instance, trailers—even little utility trailers for hauling kayaks—are subject to a small annual registration fee, and must display a license tag. If the trailer weighs less than 2,000 pounds, in Florida it's not subject to title requirements, but that might not be the case in other states.

Before buying a trailer, find out what the documentation requirements are for your state. Make sure you save them. Also check to ensure the trailer lighting conforms to state regulations. Adding the correct lights is not a difficult job.

Trailex, a 50-year-old manufacturer of utility trailers based in Ohio, includes an MSO (Manufacturer's Statement of Origin), VIN (Vehicle Identification Number) and weight slip on all its products—even the small utility trailers. You may or may not need all of these various forms when you go to register your trailer, but you'll certainly want to keep them handy for the future. Having all the documentation (including your receipt, of course!) will make life a lot easier in the event you move to a new state, or opt to sell your trailer.

Before buying a trailer, find out what the documentation requirements are for your state. Make sure you save them.

Roof Racks

The sequence illustrates a moderate back-saving technique to load a kayak on a roof top using a Yakima Boat Loader.

Yakima has a great website that allows you to instantly customize and configure rack systems for nearly any vehicle. One handy accessory, compatible with the company's Round crossbars, is the Boat Loader—an extendable arm that slides out of the hollow crossbar. With the Boat Loader in place, you can stabilize one end of the kayak while lifting the other to place it on the opposite crossbar. Josh Harvel, a kayak guide in Southwest Florida, loads a 13-foot Hobie Revolution that weighs 58 pounds unrigged. Without the Boat Loader, he'd have to either slide the kayak up the rear crossbar, or balance it overhead. Either way, you risk scratching the vehicle or herniating a disc, or both!

Fishing salt water? Rinse the kayak before loading, and wash your vechicle after every excursion. Note this rusted windshield frame on a Nissan Pathfinder. Veteran kayaker Jerry Mc-Bride, below, built a reservoir for rinsing on the spot.

A Central Florida resident and longtime contributor to *Florida Sportsman magazine*, Jerry McBride came up with a great way to build a fresh-water wash-down that can be hauled in the back of a truck. He used a 10-gallon round livebait well, and installed a 12-foot hose. Alligator clips to the truck battery power up a pump that propels clean, fresh water onto the kayak as well as fishing gear.

Hully rollers compatible with Yakima crossbars allow you to roll the kayak onto the roof.

Sweet setup: Overhead storage keeps rods and lines from tangling, and preserves space for other gear.

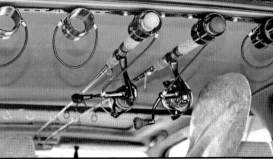

Pickup the Slack

Pickup trucks present something of a conundrum: On the one hand, you can slide a kayak right into the bed, side-stepping some of the corrosion and cosmetic issues faced by roof-toppers. On the other, that kayak might stick out too far.

Owners of compact pickup trucks might find a solution in the anodized aluminum Xsporter system from Thule: The mounting rails clamp onto the top of the truck bed, and the vertical supports may be adjusted for height as desired (definitely keep the forward portion of the kayak elevated above the roof of the cab). The Xsporter is rated for 450 pound loads, which is way more than two kayaks will account for.

Whether you're using a bed extender or just securing the boats in the truck bed, be sure to consult with your state Department of Motor Vehicles for marking and lighting requirements. In Florida, for instance, loads which project 4 feet or more beyond the truck body must be marked with 12-inch-square red flags during daylight hours, and red lamps and reflectors for nighttime.

Laws also dictate what should be obvious: That load must be secured. There are ratcheting tie-downs that can be affixed to eye straps on the kayak.

Last but not least, a van or large sport utility vehicle may well carry your entire rig out of sight. Such is the case with your author's 9-foot mini kayak, which fits into the back of

Pickup beds will accommodate kayaks, but make sure they're marked and well-secured, right.

A van or large sport utility vehicle may carry your rig out of sight. Floor mats and pre-loading washdown are good ideas!

You see a lot of these Thule Xporter units on compact and full-size pickup trucks. They preserve bed space, and open up countless options for customization.

A bed-extender may be mounted in a trailer hitch receiver. One system, from Haul-Master, was selling for about $50; Florida kayaker Greg Timmer added a set of LED tail lights, and hired a mechanic to cut and re-weld a slight angle in the extender, to avoid bottoming out on inclines. He also added Yakima Land Shark supports to cradle the kayak. (Pictured wheels and gear will be removed, of course, and kayak lashed securely before hitting the road.)

a Suburban. The saltwater launches I frequent are equipped with outdoor showers, a very important step before loading my kayak into my truck. When your better half gets in and announces "Your truck stinks!" that's a reminder to take better care of your gear.

Rugged plastic mats are always a good upgrade if you're carrying kayaks or gear inside. I have a big plastic cloth that can unfold to cover the entire back two-thirds of the truck, plus a plastic bin to contain wet boots, clothes and towels. But eliminating salt and gunk is essential.

Rare is the day my kayak sees a roof rack—and then only the factory-mounted Chevy rack. To cushion the kayak and minimize slippage, I zip-tie foam plumbing insulation to the crossbars, then lash the kayak down with flat nylon straps. For long trips, I always make at least one additional fail-safe connection: Run a short, 1/4-inch nylon rope through a kayak scupper and tie the whole kayak—firmly but not placing any immediate stress on the scupper—to the roof rack. At my destination I'll unlash and unbuckle the standing straps, but usually I'll have to knife through the safety line. No big deal. With any of these systems, the point is to avoid any possibility of losing the kayak on the highway, triggering a potentially tragic chain of events. Extra lashings to the front and rear bumper are similarly advisable, in the unlikely event the roof rack itself fails.

Keep Rolling to the Water

So you've reached the lake or beach with your kayaks safely lashed to the roof, trailer, or truck bed. You're still not there yet: You may have to cover another 200 feet to the water with a 50-plus-pound kayak.

That's where wheels and carts are hugely valuable. Not only can you convey your boat to the water without straining your back or dragging the hull, you can do it with a loaded boat, minimizing the back-and-forth trips.

Some guys lash the cart to the back of the kayak. Another option is a collapsible model, such as the Wheeleez kayak cart—with the detachable wheels (pneumatic or foam-filled), the Wheeleez might sneak inside the forward storage of your kayak, certainly the case with the big oval compartment on a Wilderness Systems kayak.

Convey your boat to the water without straining your back, and do it with a loaded boat, minimizing the back-and-forth.

Nylon strapping ensures the kayak won't slip off on inclines or while wheeling over unstable terrain.

Home-built PVC roller can be customized for any vessel at a fraction of the cost of name brand carts. This particular one uses pool noodles for traction on the hull of the kayak. Also note the kick stand for ease of loading the kayak by a single person.

Oval dry storage on a Wilderness Systems kayak accommodates this collapsible Wheeleez unit.

This 120-pound Hobie is nimble on the water; not so much on land. A set of wheels is definitely a good investment.

About Those Inflatables

If you really want to ditch the load, and are expecting only a few trips per year, an inflatable kayak is worth consideration.

One problem, of course, is that you can't bolt on rod holders and other accessories. You're limited by what you can carry inside the little craft.

But for simply stroking off toward a distant sandbar, or patrolling an interesting backwoods stream, inflatables are pretty neat.

I tested a West Marine Scout Advanced Frame Inflatable Kayak. This one folds up into a 32-pound package that you could transport as luggage on an aircraft. It also fits easily into the trunk of a compact car.

The Scout comes with a bellows-type inflating device—you simply attach the hose and pump up four chambers—the main body, the inflatable floor, and two support members. It takes only a few minutes, and suddenly you have a 10-foot kayak! With internal aluminum frame pieces, the Scout is surprisingly rigid and fun to paddle. Of course, it's a sit-inside kayak, meaning it's not self-bailing. So you'll want to avoid rough water.

Hobie Cat makes a series of PVC, rigid hull inflatable kayaks, from a 9-footer up to a tandem 14. Company Director of Engineering Jim Czarnowski showed me some photos he'd taken on a summer trip to the Kenai River region of Alaska.

"My wife and I have taken this trip the last two years in row—we take the inflatable kayaks on the plane, then keep them in the rental car," said Czarnowski. "When we see a stretch of river we like, we pull out the kayaks and fish! You can drag this kayak over rocks; it's pretty darn durable. The material is made out of PVC, with hundreds of little fibers. It's rigid, hardly flexes at all." SB

Hobie Cat makes a series of PVC, rigid-hull inflatable kayaks, from a 9-footer up to a tandem 14.

Author looks a little uncertain as he prepares to test an inflatable kayak. Is there really a boat in there?

The whole kit emerges from the stuff sack, and assembles in minutes.

A bellow-style foot pump inflates the hull compartments. Suddenly, a kayak appears!

Not as well-outfitted as some of the vessels in this book, but can you do this with your kayak?

For paddling to a sandbar or patrolling a backwater stream, inflatables are pretty neat.

CHAPTER 8

Bass Fisherman's Magic Carpet Ride

To a diehard bass fisherman, the connection should be obvious and irresistible—a small lake or slow river, with downed timber or heavy vegetation, would be difficult to navigate with an electric motor, let alone a big outboard. There may or may not be a boat ramp, or any access to speak of. You may pass that waterway on the way to work each day, wondering of the possibilities. Or, it may exist only as a creative extension of your mind, populating that tiny blue dot on the map with giant green bass that have never seen a lure.

More than simply an affordable alternative for the thrifty bass fisherman, a thoughtfully chosen kayak solves some compelling problems. Yes, you can simply plop AOK (any old kayak) in a lake, take a rod and a box of lures, and go bass fishing. But there are some strategic considerations you'll soon face.

You may pass that waterway on the way to work each day, wondering of the possibilities. Let's explore the freshwater lakes, ponds and rivers.

Heavy pad cover, right, makes things tough on powerboats. Not so the kayaker. Good catch, above.

Where Powerboaters Fear to Tread

One advantage of the kayak is access. Backwater ponds and hidden oxbow lakes may be the last frontier of North American bass fishing. What makes them so unique, often, is that fishermen are unable to launch a powerboat there. The same holds for larger lakes during periods of drought. In North Central Florida, a number of A-list bass waters went largely unfished for almost a year in 2002. Ramps were high and dry, and the fish were concentrated —and hungry!—in pockets of open water. Similarly, marsh impoundments managed for water storage and/or flood control are often left deliberately undeveloped by authorities.

If a clean trail is available, you might wheel a full-size, fully equipped kayak down to the water's edge, launch and be on your way. If some measure of bush-whacking or elevation change is in the picture, you might consider a light-weight mini-yak. I have a 9-footer that weighs in at about 40 pounds unloaded; I can carry it easily with one hand, two if I'm in a hurry and making a nonstop trek with a basic assortment of tackle inside. On wet-hikes through sawgrass or other marshy areas, I rig a ¼-inch nylon rope with a big loop in one end, and sled the kayak behind me until I reach open waters.

It's a kick when you bust through cover to find a piece of water all to your-self. Bass in these small waters tend to be much less finicky than those on headline lakes that see some tournament or another every week. Gear capacity isn't as much of an issue, if you're working a lake which consists of a midlake trough of 6 or 7 feet, perimeter spawn-ing flats in the 2- to 4-foot range, and perhaps a few re-stricted areas of inflow and outflow. Sonar in water this shallow is of limited utility. And a quiver of rods isn't really necessary.

Author on a central Florida marsh with no boat ramp access. His basic spring-summer box, left.

Two rods might suffice, one rigged for probing deep water with a crankbait or Carolina rig, and the other set up with a topwater, spinnerbait or weedless fluke for working shoreline cover.

And of course here is where we take a brief detour from the paddling world, to consider for a moment the modern bass boat. Bass fishing has evolved from simple one-rod, one tackle box pursuit into something akin to golf. Anglers in search of tournament riches or local bragging rights now think nothing of taking 8 or 10 fully rigged rods and reels, and strapping them to the front deck. The televised tournaments really have helped drive this trend, much to the benefit of tackle companies, and sometimes to the benefit of anglers. The ability to quickly reach for a backup bait, say a soft-plastic, to plop in front of a bass that swirled on a topwater certainly puts the odds in your favor. And with a bow-mount trolling motor integrated with a sonar screen up front, the fisherman has unparalleled situational awareness and control.

All this comes down kind of hard on the humble kayak fisherman, whose domain is restricted to 10 or 13 feet of narrow polyethylene and what propulsion he can make for himself. Lifting off at 60 mph, to head for the far end of the lake, may seem a tantalizing dream. But that dream is in many ways a fog. The window of the kayak fisherman is not so two-dimensional; it's actually richer, as the paddler learns to more thoughtfully consider such variables as wind, water temperature and micro-ecosystems. If that calm western shoreline isn't producing, the kayaker eventually figures out how to make it produce, while the powerboater might race off to the horizon.

This is not to say the kayak is too limited. Dedicated bass fishermen have come up with some ingenious ways to maximize tackle storage and optimize performance on the water. Philip Ruckart typifies the true kayak basser. Philip hosts guided fishing trips in the Piedmont region of North Carolina, as well as saltwater trips to the Beaufort area. When he's not fishing, he works in video production for North Carolina State University School of Veterinary Medicine. Philip doesn't wear patches on his shirts, and he doesn't yell at the fish.

There may be a sandy beach, below, but untapped waters may require a wet-hike, left.

"Big Block Super Sport of Bass Yaks"

That's what a tarheel gentleman exclaimed upon seeing Philip's kayak, before we launched in mid July on Randleman Reservoir outside of Greensboro, NC: "You've got the big block super sport!"

Waters like Randleman represent a sort of new frontier for kayak fishermen, to the extent that it's managed solely for the purposes of water supplies for a metropolitan area. There's a fine boat ramp at Southwest Park, but the ramp and adjacent waters are off limits to combustion engines. An 8-year-old reservoir at the time, Randleman was in a prime period in the life cycle of a bass lake. Sunfish and other forage species had become well-established, as had vegetation. Bass had learned to move to midlake channels to escape summer heat, taking up residence in prime areas adjacent to feeding zones. Water quality was excellent, as one would expect for a water supply storage.

"Geologically, lakes of the Piedmont are clay bottom," said Philip. "We don't have lots of mineral rich soil, like upstate New York or Washington state. And we don't have big ledges. We kind of depend on lakes with some structure, whether it's ditches or natural blowdowns, to create fish-holding areas. We have a lot of these reservoirs; you can almost think of them as large ponds."

The ramp opened at 6 a.m., which left us racing to beat the sunrise; afternoon temps were expected in the mid 90s.

"Around here, after the spring spawn, a lot of people think it's too hot to fish. But 10 feet down, the water temp might be 72 degrees, when it's 92 on the surface. We'll look for deeper, more sudden drops, which present for bass an easy opportunity to come up to feed on baitfish, then easily migrate to deeper water. Because it's warm, bass metabolism is in higher gear; they're more active this time of year than people realize."

To the gee-golly of a few locals, Philip and I hauled down to shore his vessel of choice, a Native Watercraft Mariner 12.5 Propel. The Mariner is a sit-on-top kayak 32 inches wide; a reasonably agile fisherman can stand and cast, or propel the boat with a pushpole, sight-fishing

> **To escape summer heat, bass move to channels adjacent to feeding zones.**

across spawning beds. What's perhaps more intriguing, the Mariner is equipped with Native's trademark Propel drive. This system is like a fusion of a bicycle with a trolling motor—that is if the bicycle had a reverse gear. The gearboxes and shaft are enclosed in an aluminum housing. The prop, injection-molded plastic, turns at a ratio of 10:1, ten revolutions per complete pedal stroke.

In bass fishing, as in saltwater snook fishing and some other venues, a hands-free option for reverse can come in very handy.

Minutes after we cleared the beach, I watched as Philip went through the bass fisherman's process of deduction; though 800 miles from my home waters,

More than meets the eye: There's a milk crate hidden inside a Precision Pak cover. Rubber risers keep the storage box above the tankwell. The Scotty rod holder bases are mounted on aluminum angle brackets. Philip's ingenuity.

A reasonably agile fisherman can stand and cast, sight-fishing spawning beds, for instance.

Philip Ruckart (holding bass above) makes good use of a Native Mariner: Pedaling across open water, top left, and standing to fish structure.

Even 10-pound braided line can exert an amazing amount of pressure on a fish.

I recognized his shifting from topwater lure, to Texas-rigged plastic, to spinnerbait. The spinnerbait did the trick, on a spunky if not quite tournament-worthy bass. The fish struck near a

ing Bubba, but still that 10-pound can exert an amazing amount of pressure on a fish… and a boat. A bass can indeed pull a kayak, at least far enough to win the match in some cases.

Regardless of propulsion system, most kayaks can be rigged to play the game reasonably well, either with a stake anchor (for shallow water) or a small mushroom or collapsible grapnel, for deeper waters.

Clockwise: Adjustable RAM base for display; 12-volt, 7-amp-hour APC battery in a sealed box; transducer (blue tape) mounted with Lexel adhesive. Bungee in foreground holds the battery box (connectors for power terminals shown).

pile of downed timber (adjacent to a 12-foot deep channel apparent only on the fishfinder screen), and immediately Philip back-pedaled to gain traction. There's a reason why bass fishermen don't obsess about screaming drags and 100-yard runs… and it's not necessarily a reflection on the fighting qualities of the target species. It's just a simple truth that many bass will get away, if allowed to burrow into a mass of branches, lily pads or hydrilla. Philip uses mostly 10-pound braided line, quite a bit lighter than the Saturday morn-

For times when he wants to stay put for spell, Philip has a 5-pound, plastic-coated mushroom anchor at hand, with nylon line wrapped around a Christmas tree light wheel.

A nylon cord at boatside has a ring which can guide the anchor line fore or aft, as conditions warrant. A zigzag cleat makes fast the anchor line at the desired length, and allows for quick release if necessary.

"If I'm fishing rivers in higher current, I clip on a rescue knife as an emergency cutaway—you never know when you'll have a build up of grass on the

Sport Fish for Kayakers

Largemouth Bass
(*Micropterus salmoides*)

◆**A.K.A.** Black Bass, Green Trout
◆**Range:** Throughout contiguous United States and northeastern Mexico, though native only to eastern U.S. Mainly lakes, reservoirs and slow-moving rivers and streams.
◆**Size:** 1 to 3 pounds common. World record 22 pounds, 4 ounces.
◆**Diet:** Whatever fits inside their mouth: insects, small fish, large fish, amphibians.
◆**Kayak Tactics:** Will vary depending on watershed and time of year. General tips: Fish spinnerbait or crankbait near edges of structure or around baitfish schools. For thick vegetation, pitch soft-plastic worm or weedless jig into holes, or skim the surface with weedless fluke or toad-style plastic. Standup-capable kayak useful for sight-fishing during spring bedding season.

Bare-bones mini kayak may be all that's needed in a shallow, backcountry pond.

line, and suddenly it gets heavy; that can be dangerous if you get a rolling wave."

Philip carried four rods, a respectable quiver for bass fishing. Sticks not actively in use are carried in vertical rod holders built into a Precision Pak milk crate cover, a neat piece of gear that gives shades to lure boxes, cell phones and other gear.

Behind his seat, he mounted a pair of Scotty rod holders on 11-inch risers, farther back than typical stock rod holders on a fishing kayak.

"You want the rods within natural reach, easier than grabbing them right behind your back."

Philip's fishfinder, an Eagle 250, is powered by a 12-volt, 7-amp-hour battery—"basically a computer APC or backup battery," housed in a water-resistant box. The power cable emerges through a rubber grommet supported by epoxy. The battery fits inside the forward hatch, near the shoot-through transducer, which itself is cemented into place in a flat spot using Lexel.

"It's a pretty flexible adherent, bonds well with polyethylene," Philip said. "It's important that when you set it in, you work it down, to squish out any air bubbles that might interfere with a good signal."

Spinnerbait nabs a channel-edge largemouth.

Rivers and Streams

Paddling and fishing a backcountry pond or calm reservoir is a fairly simple affair, and as we've seen the tactics and gear aren't far removed from what you'd employ from a powerboat.

Flowing water presents some unique challenges. Also some rewards.

Let's define flowing water, for now, as water swift enough to be an inconvenience, carrying your kayak past fish-attracting structure before you can effectively fish it—but not so swift that a swimmer of average ability cannot extricate himself, and his gear, from trouble.

True whitewater kayaking, as already indicated in the introduction, is a thrilling sport, and opens up some new horizons for intrepid anglers. But first you'd need to seek hands-on, certified instruction,

as well as gear advice, which is beyond the scope of this book. The American Canoe Association (www.americancanoe.org) is a good source. Also, American Whitewater (www.americanwhitewater.org) is a river stewardship and safety advocacy group with a wealth of information—including river level classifications and sobering records of how things can go wrong, quickly, on fast water. World Kayak (www.worldkayak.com), founded in 2007, focuses on whitewater education through its Ambassador program.

For many streams and rivers, however, sit-on-top kayaks, spinning gear, and summer afternoons are a combination made in heaven.

Drew Gregory, a professional kayak fisherman in Charlotte, NC, grew up fishing creeks and rivers of the southeastern U.S. Early on he became fascinated with the black basses of moving water, especially the shoal bass and smallmouth.

"They tend to fight the hardest of the bass

> Poster child for river bassin', Drew Gregory swings up a smallmouth on a remote Canadian stream.

The Coosa kayak, set up for drift-fishing rivers, was conceived with Gregory's advice and the whitewater expertise of Jackson Kayak.

species," he said. "And I like the seclusion and the scenery—you're seeing eagles, otters, beavers. Shoal bass, for instance, tend to live in swift water—around waterfalls, boulders, places inaccessible to motorboats. I like to throw big swimbaits—either plugs or soft-plastics—into calm spots in the middle of rapids.

"For smallmouth bass, I'll use something like a Zoom Fluke or Strike King Zulu on a weighted hook. Throw into shoals and rocky areas, and reel the bait so it skips quickly on the surface."

The foregoing advice begs the question: How do you slow and stabilize the kayak while casting to likely lies?

Among Gregory's contributions at Jackson Kayak are fisherman's design concepts such as the aft recesses molded into his signature Coosa model kayak. The Coosa is an 11-footer, just over 31 inches wide, with a slight rocker to enable maneuverability in tight quarters. The recesses are designed to cradle a drag chain, an 18- to 24-inch length of sturdy chain weighing 2 or 3 pounds. The chain may be tied off to the end of a retractable dog leash for convenient deployment. The weight and friction of the chain (typically encased in Gorilla tape or a plastic bicycle tube) slows and in some cases stops the kayak.

"You always want to use the drag chain straight off the stern," said Gregory. "And here's a good rule of thumb: If the water is too swift for you to back-paddle—meaning paddle yourself backwards upstream, it's probably too swift to anchor. If you get the chain stuck, you'll need to paddle upstream."

When passing through swift, rocky sections of a river, it's safest to retrieve the chain and focus on paddling.

"Learning about paddling is really the key to fishing moving water—good positioning requires good boat control—and that's where professional instruction comes in," he said. "Here's an example: You might suddenly see an obstacle in front of you, and instinctively paddle on your right side to go left, around it... but with the current moving you in that direction, the boat turns broadside, and now you're only moving faster toward the obstacle. If you'd simply back-paddled in the left side, slowing yourself down, you'd still be turning to the left, and then you could've made forward strokes away from the obstacle.

"Things like this you learn from instruction and experience. You have to know and respect your limits, and work your way up in skill levels."

The same can be said for fishing tidal waters, and finally, the open sea, where we'll find ourselves in subsequent chapters.

> Positioning is the key to fishing moving water, and that's where instruction comes in.

Great Lakes

Now here's lake fishing that more closely resembles sea kayaking: Trolling the clear, cold waters of the Great Lakes for salmon and steelhead.

Salmon and steelhead, both introduced to the Great Lakes, have long provided excellent sport and fillets for anglers aboard powerboats. The standard drill is to troll spoons, flies or plugs, usually with several lines set at different depths.

While it's difficult for a kayaker to replicate the spread, let alone cover the miles of open water sometimes demanded, there are times of the year when kayaks are terrific vessels for surgical strikes.

Chris LeMessurier lives in Bloomfield Hills, a suburb of Detroit, Michigan. He runs a kayak fishing website and guide services dedicated to the Great Lakes region (www.kayakfishthegreatlakes.com).

"Fall is really the best salmon season here, especially from the kayak. The fish move closer to shore, as they return to the tributaries," he explained. "Certain parts of the Great Lakes, where it drops off quickly, we're only paddling out a couple hundred yards from shore, into 40 to 60 feet of water. The fish may be throughout the water column.

"We use sonar, try to mark fish and bait. I use a simple setup—a rod off to the side, troll-

ing a big lipped crankbait, like a Rapala or Storm that dives 18 to 25 feet. We might also use dipsy divers [an adjustable, planer-like device], maybe experiment and pull spoons, J-plugs, similar to what guys do from boats.

"One advantage we have in a kayak is, many powerboats actually have a hard time going slow enough to troll effectively. Two, 2 ½ mph is a comfortable kayak stroke ... you go out for a paddle, get some exercise, and before long you're loading up with fish!"

If the word "comfortable" doesn't fit your image of paddling on the Great Lakes, Chris notes that the summer and early fall weather is often balmy.

The steelhead is a seagoing strain of rainbow trout native to the northern Pacific Ocean. Hatchery-raised specimens, whose genetics stem from western U.S. watersheds, have been continually stocked in Lake Michigan and other Great lakes for more than 100 years. Some natural reproduction takes place in cold, pristine tributaries of these Lakes. They are powerful sport fish. This fish, estimated at 10 pounds, is being released by Chris LeMessurier, who was fishing the White River in Ontario, Canada. Photo by Jared Walega.

While salmon make their way shoreward during the September transitional period, there are often Indian Summer-type days with air temperatures in the mid 70s. There are different schools of thought on vessel design in this part of the country, but many kayakers are now leaning toward sit-on-top vessels. They'll layer up with paddling pants or breathable waders, perhaps even a dry suit on a really cold day.

There are many other options for kayak fishing in this region. When he's not on the lakes, Chris and his buddies might be found paddling local rivers for winter or spring steelhead, or resident brown trout.

"Some rivers you can paddle and fish from the kayak, trolling to cover water," he said. "Or, we might use the kayak to 'spot hop,' floating downstream, where we get out and fish spots that look the most promising."

on freshwater lakes. Let's check out the coldwater scene.

Austin Freshour fights a king salmon (two shown bottom left) on Lake Michigan, out of Glen Arbor, MI. Kayak is a Wilderness Tarpon 160. Photo by Chris LeMessurier.

Chris LeMessurier with 10.5-pound steelhead, Lake Michigan, Twin Rivers Wisconsin. Wilderness Tarpon 140. Photo by Paul Biediger.

Chris LeMessurier puts the fly rod to a brown trout on the Huron River, in Wixom, MI. Wilderness Ride 135. Photo by Paul Biediger.

CHAPTER 9

Coastal Bays Afloat

I t's an easy transition, going from your
first strokes to kayak fishing on a saltwater bay. Basic techniques honed on
protected backwaters, or while fishing
powerboats, will serve you well. Similar
presentations will catch fish, regardless
of whether you're fishing Florida, Texas
or Southern California.

But to become really proficient, you'll
need to understand the coastal environment, where fish move and why. Changing
playing fields will require different tactics,
and different rigging systems. By this
point in the book, you're well-equipped
with a kayak, safety gear, fishing tools and
proper attire, whether for tropical or cool-
weather regions. Let's look at some of the
systems veteran coastal anglers use to
catch a variety of fish.

**To become really proficient, let's look at some of the
systems veteran coastal anglers use to catch a variety of fish, in Florida, Texas, and Southern California.**

Josh Harvel, a guide in Ft. Myers, FL, with redfish in Ding Darling Wildlife Refuge. Top: Spartina marsh outside Jacksonville.

Finding Fish, Making them Eat

A chilly, misty day on San Diego Bay, California, finds Morgan Promnitz dialing in the corvina bite.

Bays large and small, east and west, invite kayak anglers to fish light tackle for a variety of saltwater species.

Morgan Promnitz, Fishing Product Manager for Hobie Cat Company in Oceanside, California, spent four years guiding sea kayak anglers out of La Jolla for trophy-class seabass and yellowtail. He still enjoys the ocean action, but nowadays gets a kick out of fishing 6- to 12-pound tackle, or a 6-weight fly rod, for back bay fish in some surprising quarters.

San Diego Bay, minutes from the border with Mexico, offers an interesting cross-section of fisheries: cool-water seabasses, the trout-like corvina, and some interlopers more commonly associated with warmer climes. The Bay is virtually surrounded by development—homes, the downtown skyline, Naval station, power generating plants. Still, there are quiet stretches where eelgrass grows out of sandy, rocky bottom; plovers maintain their nests.

"We catch a lot of bonefish here, mainly in deeper channels," said Morgan. "It's thought that the 1994 El Niño, which pushed up a bunch of warm water, also brought species not natural to this area, and they got trapped in there. The bay stays warmer than the ocean."

A fisherman acquainted with throwing light lures on spin tackle in Florida or Texas will feel right at home in San Diego Bay, with a few changes in tactics.

"It's hard fishing a crankbait or other lure with treble hooks in the bay," said Morgan. "We have a lot of this algae-type grass, and you'll hang up on every cast."

Small jigheads with shad- or shrimp-shaped tails, which ride hook-up, are good lures here. Also, some days Morgan throws Clousers or other flies on a 6-weight fly rod with a 250-grain sinking line.

"We fish a slower retrieve, imitating an injured baitfish or a ghost shrimp, which doesn't move like most shrimp—no fast darting. We just keep the lure close to the bottom."

Morgan demonstrated some good techniques on a cool, overcast August morning. He pitched jigs to markers or other structure for spotted bay bass. He retrieved jigs across open-water grassbeds for corvina, all the while maintaining a look out for clusters of birds which might indicate bonito or some other pelagic visitors.

I tagged along, in another Pro Angler, and had a relaxing morning sampling the different species available in southern California waters.

Those bay bass reminded me of juvenile gag grouper, which we call "grass grouper" in the estuaries of Florida. The corvina is a ringer for a silver seatrout.

Driving the coastal highway on the way to or from San Diego, one gets regular glimpses of broad, marshy lagoons in areas such as Del Mar, Oceanside and Huntington Beach. These waterways, fed by seasonal streams, represent nursery zones and spawning zones for halibut and other species. Many, unfortunately, are closed

> **Bays large and small, east and west, invite kayak anglers to fish for a variety of species.**

to all fishing, which is something of a bummer for light tackle anglers who'd likely enjoy a day of catch-and-release action close to home.

Mission Bay, up the coast a little, is somewhat similar to San Diego Bay, says Morgan. In lagoons which are open to fishing, drifting ghost shrimp on a sliding sinker rig is a super way to catch corbina. And there's always the possibility that small resident halibut (20 inches or so) are joined by 40-pounders fresh from the sea.

A common denominator between Morgan's approach to southern California intracoastal waters, and that of countless kayakers in the eastern U.S., is that much of the fishing is done while seated in the kayak itself. In the case of the big Pro Angler Morgan fishes out of, standing and casting is also feasible.

Either way, the caster, and the vessel, must be considered the same unit.

Wade-fishing is a different discipline, treated on

its own in the next chapter. For now, let's look at some of the strategies used in waters either too deep, or too murky, for effective wading.

As in bass fishing, mobility and the convenience of electronic fish-finding equipment are two obvious advantages when kayak fishing salt waters.

Morgan's vessel was outfitted with a 10-inch color Lowrance chartplotter/sounder combo, the most advanced system I've seen installed on a kayak. "It's powered with our full-size fishfinder installation kit," Morgan explained. "It has a 12-volt, 9 amp-hour gel cell battery with it." Fine details are useful for picking up the demersal species of San Diego Bay—the bottom-hugging bass and corvina.

A nice spotted bay bass for Morgan, a one-time kayak guide who now works for Hobie Cat in Oceanside, CA. Below: Jigging structure produces.

More typical of Florida's lower east coast, Greg Timmer met me one day in Indian River County, set up with a small Humminbird sounder, more of a depth indicator than anything else.

In Florida waters, your own eye is the primary fishfinder, at least in warmer times of the year when baitfish and birds are present.

Timmer had clearly put a lot of thought into his rig—a 13-foot Ocean Kayak Prowler tricked out for the southern Indian River Lagoon (he was awaiting one of the new Ocean Kayak Trident Ultra 4.7s).

For mixed-style fishing on the flats, Greg had aft-facing rod holders on the aft deck, keeping extra rods where needed.

then a shorter, 8-foot wading tether to conform to tournament specifications.

Most of the peninsular Florida bays are shallow enough that a stick anchor is all that's needed; Greg uses a 5-foot Stick It anchor pin, and connects the tether line to an anchor trolley

Between his legs, a Scotty rod holder mount carried an aluminum L-bracket Greg had fashioned to carry the Humminbird fishfinder. The power cable and transducer cables run through a small hole in the footwell. The transducer cable goes aft to the tankwell, and below decks through a special Humminbird scupper mount. The power cable plugs into a waterproof box in the main well; Greg built the power system himself, out of a watertight plastic box, with eight rechargeable AA batteries and a marine cigarette lighter connection.

Just behind his seat, a tall gasketed Plano boat box contains everything Greg needs for a day of fishing: Small trays holding softbaits, jigs and plugs; clippers; a first aid kit (Greg's a Palm Beach Gardens fire rescue lieutenant by trade); and a pair of nylon tow lines with carabiner clips at each end—a 15-foot line, and

There's a good reason why a Humminbird transducer fits so well in that Ocean Kayak: The two are owned by the same company. Power source and rod holder custom built.

Greg Timmer typifies the Florida coastal kayaker: efficient and well-prepared.

He made quick work out of some handsome seatrout over turtle grassflats. All of this while staked out in a 10- to 15-knot breeze, and negotiating tackle changes out of a 13-foot kayak. On this particular day I happened to be observing Greg from the deck of my 19-foot outboard flats skiff. The difference in sound profile, between my big boat, and Greg's kayak, was remarkable. At one point a school of redfish dropped into the hole Greg was anchored up in. The fish milled about the kayak as if it were not even there (unfortunately a feisty blue outraced the reds to Greg's lure!).

installed on the starboard side of the kayak. It's a convenient system for adjusting the angle of approach; in most circumstances, putting the stake anchor directly forward or aft of the kayak is best, to minimize wave and current effects on the hull. A section of foam pool noodle on the Stick It shaft ensures the device isn't lost.

"Over the years I've had a bunch of power-boats," Greg told me. "Now I'm totally on the plastic Navy!"

Greg's system was a model of efficiency. I watched him deftly bring a bluefish boatside, and control the toothy fish with a plastic gripper.

Much as on a freshwater lake, anchoring, strategic drifting and pedal power are some of the modes in which kayak fishermen approach open bays.

A unique situation develops in extremely shallow, clear water where redfish or bonefish are apt to forage in high alert. When these fish nose down to uncover a crab or shrimp, they often poke a portion of their tail above the surface. Focused on a meal, they temporarily let their guard down. But in a flash, it's eyes up and senses fully geared for ospreys, sharks and other predators. Tailing fish are a thrill to target, and kayaks offer some unique advantages.

Plastic lip-gripper makes safe work of a toothy bluefish.

At right: Staked out comfortably off the bow.

In most cases, putting the anchor directly forward or aft is best, to minimize wave and current effects.

This young kayaker dazzled readers of *Florida Sportsman Magazine* in May, 2012.

Dean Thomas, a kayak fishing guide in Aransas Pass, Texas, spends much of the spring, summer and fall hunting tailing redfish in the lush beds of seagrass that color the wide-open, hypersaline bays of Texas. These fish are extra spooky, Thomas says, and sensitive to the approach not only of powerboats, but even the subtle pressure waves and crushing sounds of feet on the bottom.

"I prefer to stay seated in the boat," said Thomas. "In crystal clear, super shallow water, being mobile and silent is a big advantage. What we'll do is turn sideways in the kayak, and put feet over the side to control the boat. You use your toes to sort of walk the boat forward or back, to get into position."

Thomas says the Texas reds are opportunistic feeders when they're up on the flats. These are 20- to 30-inch sub-adults fattening up for their mature years, when they'll leave for the open Gulf of Mexico.

"They'll eat a wide variety of flies and lures," said Thomas. "But in that super shallow, thick grass, you'll either need a topwater lure or, if it goes down, a weedless lure or one that runs with the hook-point up—like the D.O.A. shrimp."

The real key, Thomas says, is getting into position for that one good cast—and that's where the toe-creep comes into play.

"In the winter, when we do a lot more wading and casting in deeper water, the kayak is less of a fishing tool, and just a mode of transport," he said.

Thomas not only guides anglers but runs a rental and outfitting service out of his Aransas shop, Slowride. "I've watched the kayak fishing grow and grow over the last 10 years. You have guys who come down and say they've read about it and want to try it. Also guys who've fished saltwater their whole lives, and see kayaking as a way to get off the bank.

And then you have guys in motorboats, who try to fish the shallowest areas you can get to. The kayak takes them to that next range."

Also, there's a different kind of mobility that makes paddling the Texas bays so attractive: The ability to load up and drive to new waters.

"There's so much access here," said Thomas. "We run big, low-profile kayaks to contend with the constant wind—I have a Tarpon 160—but normally we're fishing within sight of the truck. If you want to move a mile or more, you just paddle back to the truck, load up, and drive down the beach. Where you park, you're looking at endless miles of super shallow water, and a lot of it's prohibitive to powerboats. From Rockport all around to Port Aransas, there's tons of free access."

> ## "We'll turn sideways in the kayak, and put our feet over to control the boat."

You'd be smiling, too: For Dean Thomas, in Port Aransas, TX, sneaking up on tailing redfish is about as fun as it gets.

Structure

A big redfish has no problem dragging a 12-foot kayak into the trouble spots.

If you're going to be fishing for hard-pulling species around close structure, you'll need to give some thought to an anchor system.

Mangrove terrain in Southwest Florida is a perfect example. As tides move higher, redfish, snook and other species draw closer to the thicket-like prop roots of the red mangroves that line many shores. It's tantalizing paddling a mangrove shoreline, looking for pockets beneath the overhanging limbs; points where dead wood lie stretched into open water. As quiet as you are, you're likely to notice things a powerboater might miss—such as a big redfish cruising outside the shadows of the mangroves. Pitch a soft-plastic jerkbait or shad-tail jig into these fishy areas, and you're on!

Trouble is, you're also on the way—into trouble. A 10-pound redfish has no problem at all dragging a 12-foot kayak toward the bushes, and once your line hits the barnacle-encrusted mangrove roots, it's game over.

If the depth doesn't permit wade-fishing (see next chapter), the kayaker's solution is to first place an anchor, such as one of the stake anchors described in the Accessories chapter. Ensure the anchor is secure enough to provide enough resistance to hold your ground after a hookup.

Hold Your Ground

Many kinds of anchors are available for different types of substrate. In an area where you don't wish to make permanent anchorage, a simple weight such as the downrigger ball at right can be used. Below is a folding grapnel-type anchor, which collapses for easy storage on a kayak. Angler Danny Cabo, at bottom right, picked off a nice redfish while fishing a lighted dock. You definitely need to "stand your ground," if you hope to pull a big fish away from barnacle-encrusted dock pilings.

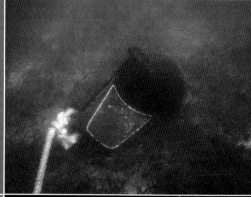

1 Josh Harvel sets up to fish mangrove shoreline.

2 He drops a stake anchor through an aft scupper.

3 Make sure the stake is planted firmly.

4 Now when a redfish crushes that topwater, Josh is ready!

Sport Fish for Kayakers

Common Snook
(Centropomus undecimalis)

◆**A.K.A.** Snook, Linesider
◆**Range:** Western Atlantic and Gulf of Mexico south of the freeze line. Among U.S. continental and territorial waters, abundant only in lower Florida peninsula, southern Texas and Puerto Rico.
◆**Size:** Average 3 to 15 pounds. World record 53 pounds, 10 ounces.
◆**Diet:** Shrimp, crabs, finfish.
◆**Kayak Tactics:** In mangrove terrain, look for tidal current around points and cuts. Cast soft-plastic bait or live pilchard. Be sure to anchor securely or wade, as large snook can easily pull a kayak and escape into the abrasive root systems of the mangroves. At night, snook may be targeted near lighted docks and bridges using flies, lipped plugs or live shrimp. Special attention to kayak safety and visibility is vital. Beware of sharp gill covers.

Snook keep falling for Mark Nichols and his plastic baits. Will they ever learn?

Keep It Simple

In the excitement of planning an inshore kayak fishing trip, there's always the temptation to load up extra rods. And while there are certainly accessory systems available to accommodate extra sticks, a basic quiver of two fishing rods should accommodate most any conceivable scenario.

Modern fishing tackle is very dependable. The days of breaking off reel handles, stripping gears and snapping rods are mostly a thing of the past, even with entry-level price point gear. In salt water, there are many good rods and reels available at the $100 level, for each component. And worries over being stripped of your line by a large fish are mostly unfounded—it's terribly difficult for a fish to spool a kayaker, if only for the simple reason that the vessel pretty much goes where the fish goes!

For warmwater fisheries, such as the mangrove bays and rivers of peninsular Florida, a basic setup would include a pair of fast-action, light- to medium-power spinning outfits in the 7- or 7 ½-foot range. If you're fishing strictly artificial lures, you might elect to set up one rod with a topwater lure, the other with a subsurface jig or spoon.

This gives you one rod in hand, a second at the ready, in the event you encounter changing conditions. Perhaps the sunlight slows the surface action, and you want to try a jig—simply rack the topwater rod and pick up the pre-rigged jig outfit.

Another common scenario, in coastal waters, is a fish that strikes at a surface plug, but fails to connect. Snook, seatrout and redfish are all notorious for doing this, and unfortunately, they're also apt to wise up after taking a swipe at a hard-plastic lure. If you get a blow-up without a hookup, quickly switch over to the subsurface rod for a follow-up cast.

Some drawbacks to bringing too many rods on a kayak:

◆Too many tangle points while casting or fight fish
◆Unneeded exposure to the elements shortens the lifespan of your gear
◆Switching among more than 2 lures at a time is usually unneccessary, and may ultimately prove counter-productive. Pick a pattern and stick with it!

The water explodes as a Florida snook tries, and fails, to take a top-water plug away from Brett Fitzgerald of the Snook Foundation. If a fish misses the hooks in this situation, it pays to have a second rod with a plastic jig, below.

Trolling

Let's look at the problem of trolling multiple lines.

Trolling spoons, jigs or small plugs is a good technique for kayak-fishing open water. It's especially useful if you aren't sure where to begin fishing, or if you're looking to mix in some sustained exercise.

Rodholder designs discussed in Chapter 4 open up a world of opportunities: You might mount a pair of outboard-angled Scottys, for instance, aft of the seat to troll two rods. Or you might put two in front of you, so you can watch the rodtips for a strike.

But slow down a moment. Let's look at the problem of trolling multiple lines.

Consider what happens when a big fish strikes. You'll put down your paddle and pick up the rod. Kayaks are amazingly efficient in the water—you happily learned that fact the first time you made

a paddle stroke away from the landing. It takes very little effort to move the boat. Don't forget that works in favor of the fish, too! As your forward momentum ceases, the drag of the fish will pull you backward ever so slightly. If it's a very big fish, that surge can be impressive. I've had 30-pound jacks literally jolt me rearward, while my hands were still working the paddle!

With the ensuing slack, if there's a second rod still in the water, there's a good chance the two lines will get crossed. Now you're in a real fix. Things get even crazier if two fish strike.

Best to stick with a single trolling line, and use the other accessory rod holders to keep appropriate casting outfits at the ready. See mackerel suddenly busting up ahead? Pick up the casting rod and fire out a jig. SB

Stroking out for the reef? No reason not to put a lure out back to catch any wandering pelagic fish.

Trolling is especially useful if you aren't sure where to begin, or you're looking to mix in some exercise.

A kayak is an efficient platform for trolling plugs, such as the shallow- and two deep-diving models shown at left. Some paddle fishermen prefer single hook lures like the one at right.

Trolling one rod keeps it simple. Set the drag loosely and attach a lanyard to the reel, for when that strike happens.

CHAPTER 10

Kayak Fishing Afoot

All this time we've been touting the merits of fishing out of a kayak, and now we're leaving our prized boats behind us. There are fishing situations which demand special attention to stealth, such as pursuing large spotted seatrout in marine waters. In other cases, you might want to work artificial lures over a tight constellation of features, for instance potholes in a grassflat. These may be times when it pays to get out of the boat. What are you going to take with you? How will you secure your kayak? How are you going to protect your feet?

Some situations require the ultimate stealth. Or, you may want to work lures over a tight constellation of features.

Redfish may slither into water that can hardly float a kayak. Anglers above take a break from paddling to stretch out.

Tactical Wading

Where depths are mostly measured in inches, and the bottom is firm enough, wading makes a lot of sense. Standing on your own two feet, you're unaffected by tide and wind. You can position yourself to make multiple casts at a sandy pothole in a turtle grassflat, for example. Or, you can stand your ground as a hard-charging redfish powers its way toward the safety of a dock.

You're also much quieter than you are under paddle power. Instead of lapping against the side of the hull, small waves pass easily around your legs.

Compared to bass and bay fishing, described in the previous chapters, the coastal flats kayak may be more of a range-extender and gear-hauler, and less of a fishing platform.

On your own two feet, you're unaffected by wind and tide, and can make repeated casts at a pothole in a grassflat.

Some kayaks are stable enough for standing, such as this Jackson Cuda with an assist strap. On a breezy day when you want stealth, however, get your feet wet, bottom left.

Such was the scenario I found myself in with Chuck Levi in Cocoa Beach, Florida. The northern Indian River Lagoon and associated Banana River are criss-crossed with bridges and dotted with small parks offering convenient launching points for paddle craft. The redfish and seatrout which inhabit the adjacent shallow, grassy waters are notoriously shy of loud engine noises. And, some days they are equally skittish of kayaks.

I met "Redfish Chuck" on a bluebird winter day—not a cloud in sight, water clear as champagne. He brought a pair of Jackson Cuda kayaks, 14-footers with frame seats and well-conceived storage. Certain elements of these boats are pictured in other parts of this book.

As we paddled away from a primitive launch, Chuck—who does some kayak guide trips in the region—described the scene.

"It's mostly sand down here, and this time of year the trout bunch up and seem to move

As we approached a shaded area indicating seagrass growth, we planted our stake poles and eased over the side.

from this corner of the river, down to these different docks. I know it doesn't look like trout water right now—the grass thickens up in summer—but they're here, and not many people know about them."

Chuck had brought a familiar arsenal—a pair of light, 7-foot spinning rods, with long-cast reels spooled with light braided line. Plano tackle boxes bungeed into aft recesses in the Cuda held small leadheads, soft-plastic grubs and jerkbaits.

We made a few casts as we drifted with the wind, and Chuck caught one small redfish. As we approached a shaded area indicating residual seagrass growth, instinctively, the two of us planted our stakeout poles and eased over the side.

The water was knee-deep, and the bottom compact and squeaky sand. Water temp was in the upper 60s. Chuck, in light polyester quick-dry pants, and I in Gore-Tex waders, felt equally comfortable.

You're On Your Feet.
Now What?

In some situations, it makes sense to haul the kayak with you as you wade. That's certainly the case if you expect to encounter any deep water, or wish to change out tackle or deposit a fresh catch in an iced fish bag. One of the terrors of coastal wade fishing is keeping fish on a stringer, where blacktips and bull sharks are liable to home in on them. With a kayak, you simply drop the fish in the bag, zip it up and get on your way.

I'll rig up a cord with snap clips, and clip the kayak to a belt loop; it comes along with me as I work docks and channel edges. Fishermen who do a lot of wading are no doubt familiar with belts that have extra rod holders. I've never found one as convenient as the rod holders in a kayak. You can make skip-casts beneath a dock with a spinning rod, then switch over to a bait-cast outfit for throwing a big topwater lure.

When the water is very clear and the fish ultra-spooky, as was the case when Chuck and I fished together, staking out the kayak and walking away from it is a smart move.

Two important rules: Always walk down-drift from the kayak, and remember to take some form of signaling device with you—a cellular phone in a watertight bag or case, or at least a whistle. It's going to be a long day when you return to a staked-out boat, only to find the wind has caused the anchor to pull, and the boat is now drifting far away. The day is exponentially longer if you're unable to reach anyone for assistance.

In skinny water, seatrout, above, and snook, right, are wary of boats and errant shadows.

Also remember to bungee your paddle in place—and if you're the forgetful sort, always use a high-contrast paddle you can locate visually in the event it blows over.

In moving water, such as a creek or river, buy yourself some extra insurance by beaching the kayak and anchoring, or tying off to a tree.

Once your kayak and gear are secured, a good approach is to wade generally downwind or down-current, and return every 45 minutes or so to weigh anchor, then paddle to begin working another sector of the water. This lets you get far enough away from the boat to reduce your overall profile, but keeps you close enough, and within range, to ensure you're not separated from your ride home.

Early into one wade, Chuck pulled a beautiful spotted seatrout from the Indian River. We'd seen several fish working the shallow water, evidently sunning themselves on the cool winter day. Fan-casting the area proved fruitless—we only spooked fish. Chuck shifted gears and began sight-casting, waiting until he had a clear shot at a good fish, before presenting the lure.

"Some days these fish lay up really shallow, and during the higher water periods, they'll cruise right up to the mangrove edge. The trout are always wary, but the reds … lot of times they'll jump on whatever you throw at them."

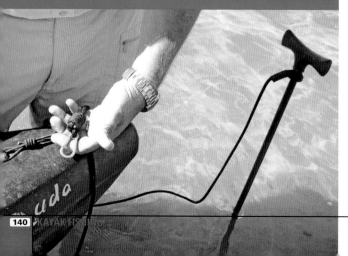

Make up various lanyards—one for your stake anchor, and one to snap the kayak to your person, if you want to haul it along.

If you choose to stake out, wade downwind of the kayak in case the anchor pulls. And don't forget to secure your paddle. Snook, like the one below, could be your prize.

Footwear

Suitable kayaking footwear is described in Chapter 6, but it's worth reminding anglers to wear protective shoes or waders while creeping across the flats. Oysters, barnacles, bits of broken shell or glass—there are all sorts of hazards out there that can ruin your day. One of the worst, in warm salt water, is the pen shell, a long, flattened, clam-like critter which buries itself so that the serrated, razor-sharp lips of its shell protrude just enough to cut you, but not enough to be easily noticed. I learned about these the way anglers do most things: the hard way. Wade-fishing with a buddy on a summer day, we both walked barefoot across what appeared to be perfectly flat sand with scattered buds of shoal grass. I noticed a few minor abrasions on the sole of my feet, but thought little of them, as I stayed busy catching redfish and pompano. Upon returning to the boat, I realized my feet were bleeding. Ribbon-like slashes looked as if I'd walked across razor blades, which in

a way, I had. Fortunately, I always keep a first-aid kit in my truck. Ample dousing of hydrogen peroxide, followed by a bandage, kept infection at bay. When I got home, I cleaned up the wounds again, and applied Polysporin and fresh bandages.

As you might guess, it's very hard tending to foot injuries on a kayak. So avoid them! SB

Boots provide little protection from the sharp spine at the base of a stingray's tail. Make sure to shuffle your feet to announce your presence and avoid stepping on top of an unseen ray. Oysters, below, definitely call for durable wading boots. Infections resulting from cuts in warm marine waters require a prompt visit to a doctor or emergency room.

As you might guess, it's very hard tending to foot injuries on a kayak. So avoid them!

CHAPTER 11

Fly Fishing

Just as there are different kayaks for different jobs, there's a functionality to fishing tackle. You select a rod to do a particular job. Are the fish taking large prey subsurface? A crankbait on a plug rod may be the best choice. Are the fish focused on very small minnows or insects in calm, clear water? A fly rod will likely be the best tool. Many anglers also enjoy the aesthetic aspects of fly fishing, either as a challenge or a reminder of local traditions. Whether you choose fly fishing for utilitarian or nostalgic reasons, you have some special considerations when selecting, outfitting or paddling your kayak.

Just as there are different kayaks for different jobs, there's a functionality to fishing tackle. A fly rod may be the best choice, in some situations.

If you can pull it off without tipping, standing up is a great way to address redfish, left, and other fly targets.

Stand and Deliver

I t just feels right, delivering a fly to a tailing redfish, while your kayak is staked out behind you. On both counts, the approach and presentation, you've forced yourself, by choice, to work a little harder than other anglers. You're as stealthy as a heron, and your senses are heightened.

Some of my own favorite paddle destinations are knee-deep tidal flats in South Florida, where gentle presentations with small patterns are best. Redfish, pompano, bonefish, seatrout, snook: Many are the species inclined to gobble up 2-inch streamer flies or crustacean patterns. Some days that's all they'll take.

In very shallow, calm water, these fish may demand precision casting and a feather-like disturbance. You can't simply fire off casts in all directions—you must pick a target. It's the saltwater equivalent of a placid run in a mountain trout stream: The fly rod is just a better tool.

But a confession: I seldom cast the fly from the kayak. I much prefer wade-fishing, using basically the same approaches outlined in the preceding chapter. I feel a sense of satisfaction transporting fly tackle aboard my kayak, but I've never been attracted to the idea of fly fishing from a seated position. Also I'm leery of high-sticking an expensive fly rod while trying to land a fish. On the other hand, fishing, much like kayaking, is a very subjective thing. What one angler dismisses as an inconvenience, another finds a gratifying challenge.

Fishing is a subjective thing. What one angler dismisses as an inconvenience, another finds a gratifying challenge.

Author enjoys pursuing redfish (bottom right) and other warm-water species by wade-fishing. He'll stake out the kayak or fasten it to his body for long walks.

Brett Fitzgerald is Communications Director for the Snook and Gamefish Foundation in Palm Beach, Florida. He's also the author of *Sportsman's Best: Snook*, and a frequent contributor of kayak fishing articles. Over the years, Brett has adapted his fly casting to fit his preferred vessel, a kayak.

"Fly fishing has forced me to take a more simple approach," he explained. "The less stuff hanging around, the better. Prep time is next to nothing—a handful of flies in my shirt pocket, a fly rod, and that's it! And I like the fact that I'm lower to the water; I feel like I can get a softer presentation."

Brett spends many days fishing tight mangrove canals in peninsular Florida. These tropical trees with long, stiltlike root systems grow out over the water to form long canopies of overhanging limbs. Snook, redfish and small tarpon are among the

The less stuff hanging around, the better. A handful of flies in my shirt pocket, a fly rod, and that's it!

species lurking around in the shady, forage rich mangrove nooks. Fly rods are great in this environment, due to the fact that you can quietly tuck casts far into the recesses, and then immediately re-position the fly, if desired, further down the line.

"I keep my casting stroke low, and my loop low—I change to more of a sidearm stroke to get flies back under the mangroves," Brett said. "I do the same thing for docks. These are areas where you often can't wade, but you don't have to cast 80 feet, either."

Chest pack and a box of author's flies for casting to tailing fish in tropical waters. Redfish, pompano and bonefish will take a similar selection of patterns.

I've already alluded to one of the big challenges facing kayak fly fishermen: landing large fish. At the end game, a 9-foot fly rod puts quite a bit of space between you and the fish. If the rod is held at too high an angle (high sticking), a sudden surge by the fish can easily snap it. On an outboard flats skiff, generally you have a second set of hands on the boat, someone to help lip or net the catch. Not so on a kayak—you're on your own.

Brett's advice: "With my rod in my left hand, I try to maneuver the fish so that it's coming from behind me, alongside my right hip. I'll either thumb the fish—a snook or bass, say—or bring it farther forward to grab it by the tail, like a jack."

Rod angle is important, and Brett outlined a triangle that helps keep stress off the fragile tip section.

"I'll hold the rod up, in my left hand, at a 45-degree angle, and my left shoulder at about the same angle. And from overhead, it would be 10 o'clock on centerline with the kayak, so the fly rod is up and forward. If I miss the fish, and he runs under the kayak, I can put the rod-tip in the water, around the front of the kayak.

"When you fly fish a lot on a kayak, you tend to isolate your arm motions. After awhile, it gets to feel awkward standing in a skiff—suddenly you have to think about your hips and shoulder."

Kayak manufacturers are catching on to the specialized needs of dedicated fly fishermen like Brett. The 14-foot Jackson Cuda, for instance, has a molded recess to accommodate the fly reel and butt section of the rod aft, with a long molded shelf running the entire length of the starboard gunnel forward. A plastic rodtip protector at the bow ensures the tip-section isn't broken while paddling through brush such as spartina grass, bulrush, cattails. These sorts of slender, pliable grasses are easily parted by a kayak yet capable of snapping a fly rod with nary a sound.

There are accessory rod holders available to cradle the fly reel and angle it in whatever direction makes the most sense while traveling.

High frame seats, as opposed to deck-level foam seats, offer a bit more elevation, which helps keep your backcast from contacting the water. This is something to consider when you're shopping for a new ride. Also, a wide-body kayak (Chapter 1), stabilizer system (Chapter 3) or paddleboard (Chapter 15) may permit standing, which most fly fishermen find far more accommodating ... to a degree. You'll need to practice casting at various angles, and picking up your line, before hitting the water with any big ambitions.

Okay, some days I do fly fish from my kayak. One scenario where I find the kayak well-suited for fly fishing is casting poppers for bass and bluegill. Here the effective range is quite short, rarely more than 30 feet. The strike is easy to read, and the fish rarely pose a hazard to the gear. You can settle a popper in a hole in the vegetation, let it lie for a minute, then give it a few strips to impart some action. If there's not strike, it's a cinch to lift it out of the water and place it elsewhere.

Fragile, expensive fly rods require special care on a kayak. Above: Molded cradle with bungees on a Jackson Cuda. Below: aft-facing Scotty rod holder.

Fly fishing from a kayak in tight quarters is a tricky thing to do. You have to consider not only possible hangups on your backcast, but what to do when a big fish strikes. Will the fish run into cover, or will it run straight at the kayak? Be prepared with a gameplan. You may need to step out of the kayak, if the water is shallow and firm enough. Or, start off from a staked position. Pedal-style kayaks are nice in that they offer hands-free propulsion—you can apply pressure against the run of the fish.

There are some big advantages, though. The kayak is super silent, which means you can slide within range of wary fish. Also, you can access waters that aren't heavily fished by motorized vessels. Fish tend to be more relaxed in places like this, and quite likely more amenable to biting an artificial fly. You're also more likely to see them if they haven't been disturbed by other boats. For fly fishermen in search of solitude and relaxing days on the water, kayaks are clearly an excellent choice. If you pay special attention to stability factors discussed in earlier chapters of this book, and carefully plan your rigging, you may find yourself preferring to fly fish from the kayak, versus wading or standing on a powerboat.

Brett Fitzgerald lays out some fly line on a stretch of Everglades canal along the Tamiami Trail in South Florida. Very good snook fishery.

Standup Fly Tampa Bay

Minimizing line-grabbers and adjusting the casting stroke help enable fly fishermen to make precise deliveries from a kayak. The style of kayak can also play a big role.

Neil Taylor is a guide and kayak fishing instructor in the Tampa Bay region of Florida. In a past life, he was a professional baseball umpire, which makes you wonder if he barks at clients for bad casts. Not so; Taylor is an easygoing guy, who, when not fishing, spends a good deal of time expressing himself on a keypad. He contributes to numerous online and print fishing journals.

Taylor, a pro staffer for St. Croix rods and Native Watercraft, primarily fishes spinning tackle, but he's helped many anglers catch their first (and second, and third...) redfish on fly.

While it's possible to catch reds by blind-casting to potholes and mangrove overhangs, sightcasting is a more efficient, not to mention thrilling, approach for fly anglers. Reds aren't as spooky as bonefish or mountain trout. They'll not only tolerate a cast delivered on their head—they will very likely to eat it.

All of which puts a premium on standup fishing ... which as we've discussed already isn't a strong point of kayaking in general.

"The trick is being able to see down into the water, with polarized glasses," said Taylor.

To enable casting from a standing position, Taylor puts fly fishermen in a Native Ultimate model, a 30-inch-wide, rotomolded hybrid kayak. A hybrid, as explained in earlier chapters,

A hybrid, such as the Native Ultimate shown here, provides some unique advantages, as Neil Taylor explains in the main story.

for catching redfish on fly in Tampa Bay.

Tampa Bay, on Florida's west coast, is hemmed in by coastal development, and yet the water is clean and full of redfish (shown) and others.

is similar to a canoe, in that the deck is enclosed by high sides. The sides help contain the fly line better than a traditional sit-on-top design. And, the width of the boat makes it less tippy.

"One beauty of that boat is it's pretty much one big stripping basket—very little things for line to get caught on," Taylor said.

An accessory rail system in the Ultimate makes it easy to remove rod holders or other potential snags.

"If they're just bringing one fly rod, I'll tell the fisherman to lay the rod in between their legs in the boat, while we paddle," Taylor explained. "If they need a second rod, I'll keep it in my boat, or it could be mounted in a Scotty rod holder aft, angled low to keep it out of the way."

The Ultimate tends to drift perpendicular to the wind, Taylor noted, which creates the right drift speed while in search mode. That eliminates the need to carry a drift chute, yet another potential snag point.

"We'll stay off the anchor, drifting until we find fish," said Taylor, "Then, when we're in 'em, we'll anchor up."

At that point, a fly fisherman can get to his feet, strip line down into the cockpit of the big hybrid 'yak, and scrutinize the water, ready to make a pinpoint delivery. SB

> **The Native Ultimate hybrid is pretty much one big stripping basket—very few things for line to get caught on.**

CHAPTER 12

Sea Kayak: West

Ocean kayak fishing is a natural extension of California's long history of waterman culture, and there's a lot to be learned from a trip out there.

Hardy salts accustomed to big swells and cold water have embarked from the harbors and rocky beaches in small outboard skiffs for decades. At the other end of the spectrum, many of the gutsiest guys would swim off the beach to dive for lobster, or spearfish halibut and other fish. A common denominator, for many, is surfing, a sport which automatically instills respect for big water, and invites a life-long challenge of the same. A surfer has little trouble judging the sets, finding the safest line out of, and more importantly back through, the surf zone.

A common denominator, for many, is surfing, a sport which automatically instills respect for big water, and invites a lifelong challenge of the same.

Mats of kelp off Santa Barbara County, CA, conceal a remarkable array of life.

Cold Water, Hot Fishing

When the fish come up the coast, they stay there off La Jolla. There's no place like it.

Kelp grows thick off La Jolla, where clear water allows deep sunlight penetration. Beach launch, top.

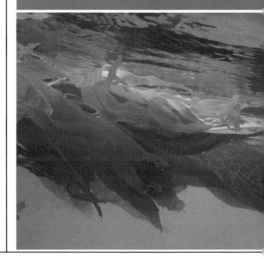

In southern California, La Jolla is perhaps the premiere destination for kayak anglers. It's a headland seated just south of the deep La Jolla Canyon. North-to-south California current pushes uphill here most days, sweeping across beds of giant kelp and bull kelp. A Florida fishermen might picture GI Joe paddling over a turtlegrass flat on an incoming tide.

La Jolla has a few other things going for it, including a flat sandy beach you can drive out on to launch. The free launch at the south end of La Jolla Shores Park is protected from south swells by the headland, and usually calm enough for fishing kayaks (see section on "Surf Launch"). Also, the nearest harbor is 9 miles away, which delays the arrival of the powerboat fleet to some extent.

Paddling out there for the first time is an exhilarating experience, as the sun slowly illuminates the rocky coastline that moments ago was sprinkled with the lights of hotels, homes and office buildings. To the north, the giant cliffs overlooking Black's Beach loom over the head of the La Jolla Canyon; this is where the North American continent literally plunges into the sea.

Andy Allen, who runs OEX Kayaks in Sunset Beach, was among the first guys to regularly fish La Jolla on a modern kayak.

"There's really no other fishery like it in southern California, even Baja … When the fish come up the coast, they stay there off La Jolla. Some days we see sheets and sheets of sardines. It's ridiculous how much life is out there."

Below is a very small but beautiful halibut.Anglers above are paddling within sight of UC Santa Barbara.

Halibut

For anglers in the heartland, halibut may be the iconic California fish. They look like flounder, as in really darn big flounder. The Pacific halibut, found mostly from the Central Coast north, may weigh over 400 pounds. The California halibut, widely distributed along the U.S. West Coast, tops out at 50 or 60 pounds.

From a kayaker's standpoint, halibut fishing is especially attractive during baitfish runs, such as the famous grunion runs. That's when the big fish slide in closer to shore, says Andy. Otherwise, you're most apt to find them on sand bottom adjacent to some structure, such as an artificial reef or rock ledge (ditto for their little Atlantic cousins, the various flounders).

Halibut fishing is best during the bait runs, when the big fish slide in closer to shore. Also try sand bottom near reefs or ledges.

One productive technique is slow-trolling with an inline sinker heavy enough to reach bottom.

A trap rig (which east coasters will know as a stinger rig) entails a single hook through the nose, followed by a short length of leader and a treble hook buried in the aft section of the bait. Halibut, again just like flounder, commonly snap at baits. That's where the rear hook comes into play. Just note that some states have prohibitions on the combination of treble hooks and natural baits.

Yellowtail

Yellowtail are a primary target along the perimeter of the kelp beds. These aren't the same thing as yellowtail snapper—in fact they're jacks, somewhat similar to greater amberjack. They're more finicky, though, and the La Jolla regulars have zeroed in on some specific ways to target them.

A nose-hooked mackerel is candy for big yellowtail and many other fish.

One is catching small mackerel on sabiki rigs, then slow-trolling them around likely areas. Like AJs, yellowtail don't have much in the way of leader-shredding teeth; unlike AJs, yellowtail are leader-shy, and 30-pound-test flouorocarbon is often used, either tied straight to the hook, or rigged with a sliding sinker and swivel.

Andy has access to many different kayaks at his OEX shop, including Malibu, Hobie and Wilderness Systems. Some of these come with factory-installed or accessory livewells. Andy uses a 5-gallon bucket with a livewell pump and intake tube that fits into a scupper. The pump is powered by battery inside a watertight case.

The green-backed mackerel are hardy baits, and the 5-gallon bucket will keep a half-dozen 6- to 8-inchers kicking for hours (surely helps that SoCal waters are cool and naturally well-oxygenated).

Sight-casting to foaming yellowtail is another specialty, wherein you try to get in position to cast a spoon across the path of the surface-feeding fish.

"If you see lots of birds, they're usually on bonito, but when we find just a few birds a ways off, moving, that's usually yellowtail," Andy said.

Yellowtail have little trouble outrunning kayaks, and so it becomes something of a thinking man's game.

"Sometimes you just pick a spot you have confidence in, and stick with it," said Andy.

Andy Allen manages a kayak shop in Sunset Beach, but shoots down to La Jolla when the yellowtail are in.

If you see lots of birds, they're usually on bonito. But when we find just a few birds a ways off, moving, that's usually yellowtail.

Steep cliffs of Black's Beach, above, hint at the spectacular dropoff close to shore. Below is a custom Humminbird portable fishfinder, and Central Coast sea kayaker Tom Reilly with a brown rockfish.

Bass

As you travel north along the California coastline, you encounter colder water, rocky headlands, giant mats of kelp.

The calico bass, or "cally," is one of the headline species up around Santa Barbara. But there are others.

On a foggy, cool summer morning, I fished out of Goleta with Tom Reilly and Mark Olsen. We launched Ocean Kayaks in calm surf, by the rickety wooden pier. The Oceans are great sea kayaks—stable, with a long internal storage space for rods, and ample carrying capacity for gear bags.

It's spell-binding poking around in the forests of kelp, and also a bit bewildering. Santa Barbara County north to Point Conception is still considered Southern California. But, it's very different from La Jolla. Not as radically different as, say, the Florida Keys from the Florida Panhandle, but close. The air

Sliding sinker rig does the trick on a calico bass.

feels heavier, the shoreline lusher. You get the sense that salmon and steelhead are migrating toward rivermouths, and in some places, they still are. Unfortunately, populations of SoCal salmonids have yet to rebound from decades of overfishing, development and pollution of coastal streams.

What remains is a colorful, and in some cas-

Friends Mark Olson and Tom Reilly launch in gentle surf at Goleta Beach.

es very tasty, mix of resident oceanic species, the basses, halibut, the rockfish, the tunas (in season), and the smelts.

Tom and Mark, both highly experienced sea and surf kayakers, are experts at negotiating the vagaries of wind and current.

Tom graduated in Environmental Studies at the University of California Santa Barbara, which happens to overlook the waters we'd be fishing. Tom runs Momentum Paddlesports, a kayak tour, fishing and instruction service in San Luis Obispo. He's also a science teacher. Mark, of Santa Barbara, is a longtime Ocean Kayak pro-staffer and a marketing rep for Tsunami.

I tagged along as these two affable, well-equipped guys stroked for a rocky headland off U.C.S.B., and we discussed our strategy.

"You'll see open lanes in the kelp," said Mark. "We'll drift through the lanes, maybe tie off and fish baits on bottom in some holes. Farther inshore," he gestured to the sandy shoreline on Goleta, "we can bounce baits for halibut."

They were prepared to fish multiple setups: One outfit with a fresh squid rigged behind an egg sinker, allowed to flutter on bottom; a second outfit, a light casting rig, can be used to fish a weedless jerkbait behind a bullet sinker. Tom also fished a somewhat heavier leadhead with a plastic shad tail, one that

Grab a stem of kelp, left, to "anchor" up, or slide your feet over, above, to slow the drift. Fresh squid, right, is a good all-around bait in the kelp forests.

thumps attractively on the retrieve.

Calico bass are wild critters, dashing up from the emerald depths to snatch lures amid the brown forests of kelp. Weedless lures, or the up-pointing hooks of the Shimano Waxwing-type jigs, are vital if you plan to work lures close to the kelp. Fishing one of Mark's Texas-rigged flukes, I felt right at home: In Florida, we use the same type lures to pull snook and redfish out of topped-out manatee grass and thick turtlegrass.

Tom emphasized safety and technique. I had reassured him of my own time in big water on the Atlantic coast, but I was nevertheless appreciative to fish with a local. As thrilling as it is, sea kayaking carries with it many dangers.

Santa Barbara kayaker Mark Olson, below, caught this fine calico bass on a piece of squid. There are many fish out west with "bass" after their name, and they're all great catches.

Florida-style bass fluke works well in the kelp.

Calicos dig the Shimano Waxwing jigs.

Bill Shedd, President of AFTCO Manufacturing Company, landed this 51-pound white seabass off Laguna, California in June, 2010. He was trolling a Rapala CD30. A white seabass hatchery in nearby Carlsbad supplies juveniles to growout pens in marinas up and down the coastline, ensuring the sustained recovery of this immensely popular fish.

Launching and Landing:
West Coast, East Coast, Any Coast

What about getting in and out of the surf? It's actually much easier getting through the waves on the way out than it is coming in. Let's look at the art of surf passage.

For starters, techniques for negotiating heavy surf are beyond the scope of this book. The reason is, you really don't want to fish in the rough stuff anyway. (Well, okay, if you're living on some remote island, fishing to feed your family, then go for it.) In some coastal towns you'll find dedicated surf kayakers who charge big waves, using specialized craft capable of drawing a line down the breaking part of the wave. This is thrilling recreation, but it isn't practical for hauling expensive fishing rods and tackle. Pick a calm day, or find a protected harbor from which to embark.

Keep in mind, ocean swells may arrive with little or no wind. Most sensible fishermen know that 15- or 20-knot winds are going to bring uncomfortable chop, but many accustomed to fishing out of deepwater harbors in powerboats aren't attuned to the effects of swell on the beach.

Data buoy reports, as well as various surf-forecasting Web services, can provide a good picture of what to expect. Six-foot waves at 6-second intervals (the time it takes for two crests to pass a given point) are obviously going to make things nasty out there, but equally worthy of concern is a very long interval swell. One- or 2-foot seas

may sound inviting, but if they're coming in at 18-second intervals, that means there's heavy water rolling under there, and that one-footer could easily become a 3- or 4-foot curling wall capable of dumping your kayak hard. It may seem counterintuitive, but the longer interval waves are moving a lot faster than the short-interval stuff. There may be longer period between their time of arrival, but once that open-ocean swell

Go West, young man. Lots of folks took that advice, and today the only way to escape the hustle-bustle of southern California is to head offshore. Even then, don't expect to be all alone. These pictures show a typical summer day in La Jolla, where folks of all ages come down to experience sea kayaking.

feels shallow water, it's bearing down on you fast.

Always assess the conditions on shore for at least 15 minutes to get an idea of the time between breaking waves. Discuss local subtleties with veterans from your area. Never be afraid to ask a lifeguard or surfer… most guys who spend time enjoying the surf want to ensure no one's injured out there.

Heading Out

The basic procedure most guys use (myself included) is to wait for a lull in the surf, then push or pull the kayak into the water until it's floating, keeping it pointing straight to sea. Hop quickly aboard and immediately begin paddling straight out. Don't be so concerned with exactly how you're sitting, or whether your pants or jacket have gotten pinched under you. It's vital to make immediate headway. Keep your attention focused straight ahead. Stroke, stroke, stroke.

If you want to keep your legs dry, and things aren't too heavy out there, you might simply line up the kayak pointed straight to sea, and step inside while the boat is lying on wet sand, where the wash comes up after each wave. You'll need to use your paddle to scoot into the arriving wash, and then be ready to stroke hard as the wash runs back out.

Coming in is trickier. You'll need to wait outside the surf zone for several minutes to time the sets (though presumably you thought about this before launching in the first place, right?). Don't attempt to catch a wave and surf it in, riding the face as you would on a surfboard. Instead, wait till a series of waves passes, and then put yourself on the back of a small one and paddle hard.

The trouble with surfing a wave is twofold: In a worst case scenario, your bow might drop (or pearl) into the trough and you'll go end over end, with unlimited potential for injury to yourself and your gear (recreational surf kayakers wear helmets!).

Pick a calm day and a beach that offers a soft landing, to practice your surf launches.

Heading back to the truck to rinse off.

Even if you manage to keep your weight back and the bow up, there's a good chance the whitewater under your aft end will cause some slippage left or right—yawing, if you will. When that happens, you must take immediate action to avoid capsizing, and that depends to some extent on what type of kayak you're in. The author's 9-foot Malibu Mini-X has very little keel forward of center, and thus it's possible to correct for side-slippage, and ride straight in to the beach, by back-paddling or dropping the blade (bracing) on the side opposite to which the kayak is turning. Not so with most longer kayaks: The keeled bow tends to dig in and resist correction. The trick here, now, is to keep the wave from rolling you. Most experts advise digging a paddle blade as deep as possible onto the wave-side of the kayak. Lean and keep your weight toward the ocean, and you'll scoot shoreward sideways. It's not pretty, but neither is the alternative.

If you capsize, anything not secured is going in the water, including your exhausted, very surprised self. In the event you go down hard, priority one is protecting your head and neck—keep your arms up when you surface. Forget about all your stuff. Invariably that corky polyethylene kayak will precede you to the beach, and you'll be left without a ship. Don't panic—conserve your energy, and with as much calm and dignity as you can muster, kick and swim yourself to the beach to recollect your boat and your pride.

Again, much better to ride up on the back of a wave, with the goal of skimming right up on the beach. But you're not out of the woods yet: Often as the keel makes contact with the bottom, there's a moment of instability, and even a small wave

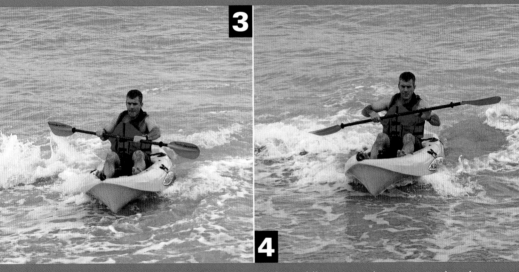

Author does a little surf training on a calm day on Florida's Atlantic coast. Here he waits for a wave to pass, then paddles up behind it, as the energy dissipates on the sand.

Make sure to come straight in, and be ready to use the paddle to control your approach and prevent capsizing. Also be ready to hop quickly out of the kayak, below, and haul it to safety before the next wave.

washing up behind you can cause the boat to yaw and roll. Again, use the paddle to straighten out the boat, and then exit, quickly, where it's safe to stand. Grab the bow lifting handle and move the boat quickly up the face of the beach to safety.

Up to a certain point, fishing kayaks are pretty good at punching through unexpected breakers, or riding up over whitewater.

Which brings up an obvious question: What is that point?

Don't put yourself in the position of wondering what you and your boat are capable of. Practice surf passages in various sea conditions, with a buddy nearby, and no swimmers in range. Leave your fishing tackle at home, until you're comfortable in the ocean. See what it takes to turn over a sit on top kayak (not much!). Learn how much energy it takes to drag yourself up the beach after falling out (a lot!). See what it feels like to get shoved under water and held down by a breaking wave (not good!).

Let Mother Nature's lessons sink in: This is potentially serious stuff. Think calm surf, protected launches, backup plans.

Spend some time body surfing or board surfing. Take lessons... Tom Reilly, featured in photos in this book, is an accredited instructor through the American Canoe Association (ACA). While attending college at the University of California Santa Barbara, he took classes on sea kayaking, and went on to become an instructor.

You'll find guys like Tom in many parts of the coastline. Ask around. Or, visit the ACA website at www.americancanoe.org. The ACA has a wealth of paddling resources, including contacts for instructors and clubs around the U.S.

Baja Peninsula, Mexico

It's an irresistible trip, one of the ultimate sea kayak fishing experiences: Paddling the placid Sea of Cortez in Mexico. But there's nothing placid about the fishing. This is a Hook Point for big-game addicts.

The stark, arid beauty of the coastline contrasts with clear, calm, warm water. Kayak rentals and modern hotels are available, and the region is a two-hour flight from San Diego. You may even find a powerboat shuttle to move you from one remote cove to another. As we've already looked at in this book, slow-trolling live bait and deep-jigging are techniques ideally suited for kayaks, and that's precisely the approach used along the leeward shores of the Baja Peninsula.

There are many interesting and different fish species to catch here, but many anglers go for the chance to catch a roosterfish or a billfish (striped marlin and sailfish, primarily).

Jim Sammons is one of the real pioneers of ocean kayak fishing. Born and raised in San Diego, he runs guided trips in southern California, hosts a kayak fishing television show, and, during the summer, arranges group trips to East Cape, near the tip of the Baja Peninsula. He's been doing the latter for about 10 years.

Bill Shedd wrangles a striped marlin to the kayak. Slow-trolling mackerel or other live baits is a good way to hook stripeys.

South of the border with Jim Sammons

Jerron Wosel scored a roosterfish on a trip to the East Cape area with Jim Sammons.

"Roosterfish are pretty fish, and ripping fast sleigh rides!"

"Roosterfish are probably my favorite," said Sammons. "They're such pretty fish, and we're generally catching them in shallow water— they have nowhere to go but out. You get on some ripping fast sleigh rides!"

Sammons says early summer, May to July, is the ideal time for large roosters (85 pounds is the biggest he's caught), but smaller specimens are present year-round.

Billfish are another of his specialties, and while they roam farther from shore, the technique is very similar—slow-trolling. Striped marlin and sailfish are in the picture from May through October.

"Slow-trolling live bait, I prefer a lever-drag reel with 50 or 60-pound braid," said Sammons. "Particularly if we get 12-inch or better mullet, mackerel or bonito. You want to troll with the clicker on, to let the fish hit and run, but you don't want the bait running out line. The lever drag lets you slide into gear just a little bit.

"It's easy paddling, just fast enough to keep the bait from swimming past you, but if a fish comes up, don't stop—sometimes you need to accelerate a little to get the bite."

Sammons says to also bring a fast-retrieve jigging outfit, a reel with a 6:1 retrieve ratio.

"Sometimes we're out on deep structure, where we'll yo-yo or speed jig, catching snapper, AJs, tuna. Fifty-pound braid is good for that, and bring a variety of leaders."

The southern Baja climate ranges from temperate to downright tropical; in summer, water temps in the Sea of Cortez can reach the mid-80s, says Sammons. It's a destination where a Florida or Texas kayaker would feel very comfortable.

"I host trips for guys who get together a group of like-minded anglers, but many of the hotels down there have kayak rentals, and there are bait pangas right out front every morning. If you bring the right equipment, you could do the trip yourself, buy a couple of baits and go."

Certainly the prospect of visiting with a veteran angler is appealing, as is the comfort of a chase boat, something with a dependable engine and shade to get out of the Baja sun. Sammons, like many of those interviewed for this book, has a web portal for his adventures, with lots of additional details about the Baja trips. You'll find it in the Resources chapter at the end of the book.

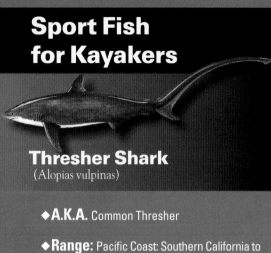

Sport Fish for Kayakers

Thresher Shark
(Alopias vulpinas)

◆**A.K.A.** Common Thresher

◆**Range:** Pacific Coast: Southern California to Panama. Atlantic Coast: Newfoundland to South Florida

◆**Size:** 40 to 140 pounds is average for inshore specimens. World record 767 pounds, 3 ounces

◆**Diet:** Finfish

◆**Kayak Tactics:** Slow-troll or drift live bait with wire leader. Threshers also frequently strike trolled or cast plugs. Very acrobatic, determined fighters; regarded as on par with billfish.

Morgan Promnitz with thresher (released) off La Jolla.

Kayak Fishermen Impacted by Marine Zones

Kayak fishermen everywhere should pay close attention to what's happened to coastal fisheries access in California. Some long-popular fishing grounds are now off-limits to all fishing, even catch-and-release. Others are restricted to the landing of pelagics only—no rockfish, seabass or other bottom fish.

Saltwater anglers hoping to bring home fish for dinner have long been accustomed to checking seasons, size limits and bag limits. We invest in the resource through fishing license fees, as well as excise taxes on fishing gear, marine fuel and other related items.

There've been major strides in fisheries management following the 1976 U.S. Magnuson Stevens Act, which restricted foreign fishing fleets from U.S. waters, and set up advisory commissions and science centers to rebuild fish stocks. At about the same time, many U.S. coastal states embarked on their own efforts to better manage local stocks. Recreational anglers, too, began uniting, successfully, to root out longstanding commercial dominance of fisheries decisions.

Today, many saltwater fish species are recovering. Tighter regulations allow more fish to spawn. Hatcheries and habitat improvements have made a big difference, for some.

However, that hasn't stopped late-arriving, well-financed environmental groups from pushing for total closures.

Early in 2012, the final installment of California's Marine Life Protection Act (MLPA) took effect, closing about 10 percent of state waters out three miles between Point Conception and the border with Mexico. The closures hit local anglers hard, especially kayakers.

"The explanation was diversity of substrate—sandy beaches, rocky headlands, kelp beds," said Greg Stotesbury of AFTCO fishing tackle in Irvine, CA. "Every area had to have a percentage makeup of different components—basically all the places you'd want to fish."

Stotesbury and AFTCO's president, Bill Shedd, were among Southern California sportsmen gasping beneath the rising tide of closures.

"The fix was in from the beginning," said Shedd. "Their goal was 10 percent of state waters; after some compromise, they got 7 or 8 percent, but because this coastline is mostly flat sand, it's

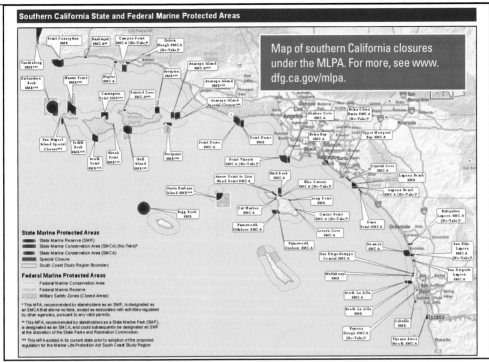

Map of southern California closures under the MLPA. For more, see www. dfg.ca.gov/mlpa.

State Marine Protected Areas
State Marine Reserve (SMR)
State Marine Conservation Area (SMCA) (No-Take)*
State Marine Conservation Area (SMCA)
Special Closure
South Coast Study Region Boundary

Federal Marine Protected Areas
Federal Marine Conservation Area
Federal Marine Reserve
Military Safety Zones (Closed Areas)

* This MPA, recommended by stakeholders as an SMR, is designated as an SMCA that allows no take, except as associated with activities regulated by other agencies, pursuant to any valid permits.

** This MPA, recommended by stakeholders as a State Marine Park (SMP), is designated as an SMCA, and could subsequently be designated an SMP at the discretion of the State Parks and Recreation Commission.

*** This MPA existed in its current state prior to adoption of the proposed regulation for the Marine Life Protection Act South Coast Study Region.

"It's really like 40 percent of the fishing areas!"

really like 40 percent of the fishing areas!"

California's MLPA was signed into law by Gov. Gray Davis in 1999. But it lacked funding until a nonprofit known as the Resource Legacy Fund Foundation (RLFF) stepped in, in 2004. Following in Davis' wake, Gov. Arnold Schwarzenegger added political muscle, in the form of a Blue Ribbon Task Force, which began shading in the proposed closures, variously termed Marine Reserves, Marine Conservation Areas, and Special Closures. The Natural Resources Defense Council and Ocean Conservancy supported closures.

Recreational angling groups attempted to roll back some of the closures, under the Partnership for Sustainable Oceans (PSO), which included the United Anglers of Southern California, Coastside Fishing Club and Bob Fletcher, a past Chief Deputy Director of California Fish and Game.

The final MLPA implementation, in January 2012, was unfortunate news for California sportfishermen, who've long supported fisheries conservation. In 1990, state anglers backed a successful ballot measure prohibiting gillnets in state waters. Longlines have been prohibited under state law for over 30 years.

White seabass have been in recovery for 10 years; a 2009 assessment by Fish and Game indicated no new management action necessary. Recreational license dollars and volunteer efforts help pump a quarter of a million of those seabass into California waters each year, through the Ocean Resources Enhancement and Hatchery Program in Carlsbad.

A species which sportsmen helped recover from the brink of commercial extinction, nurtured along through a groundbreaking hatchery program, was rendered inaccessible in many areas by the MLPA.

Calico bass is another popular species in nearshore kelp beds; many of the best areas were set for closure.

"In the last few years, environmental groups have overpowered us, stolen our conservation moniker, and they're claiming they're gonna protect the ocean the way they see best, by kicking out those of us who care most about the fish," added Bill Shedd.

To find out more about coastal closures, see www. KeepAmericaFishing.org Also, get involved with local fishing clubs, or organizations like United Anglers of Southern California, International Game Fish Association, American Sportfishing Association and Coastal Conservation Association.

CHAPTER 13

Sea Kayak: East

There are only so many inlets along the U.S. Atlantic coastline, with huge stretches of fishable waters in between them. When fuel prices rise, powerboaters feel the pinch. Not so the kayak fisherman. If the ocean is calm, he can launch most anywhere there's public access to the beach. The thrill of catching a large fish from a kayak is intense. It's an exciting approach, but one that requires careful attention to safety systems and intimate knowledge of the ocean.

Sea kayak fishing on the Atlantic coast is thrilling, but requires careful attention to safety systems and intimate knowledge of the ocean.

They really do call it the Gold Coast. Kayaking off Pompano Beach, FL, this guy knows where the real treasure is.

Little Boats, Big Fish

As in California, the U.S east coast is home to a hybrid surfer/fisherman culture that sees many guys heading through the breakers in kayaks bristling with rods.

This is actually where I got involved with kayaks in the first place. The beaches along Hutchinson Island, one of the many strips of barrier island on Florida's east coast, are within striking distance of migratory kingfish, jacks, permit, tarpon, cobia—you name it. The kayak provides a few unique advantages over a powerboat (I own both). For one, during the summer, there's usually a small window of optimal fishing, right around sunrise. The time it takes to load and launch a skiff, clear the inlet, and run to the action, can be considerable. And if you plan to be at work that morning, you have to do all this double-speed, plus figure time for flushing the engine and hosing off the boat and trailer.

With the kayak, you can simply roll up to a beach park, walk over the boardwalk or dune, and check things out. No birds here? Move along to another access point.

My truck is a lot easier on fuel than my skiff, and if it so happens I don't find any signs of fish along the beach, well, I can call it a morning and go eat a proper breakfast before work.

Many days I'll see skiffs and bay boats traveling up the beach, while I'm already returning to shore with a bag full of eatin' fish or at least some stories for the guys at the office.

I favor beaches with open freshwater showers, to give the yak, the gear and myself a quick rinse before packing up for the morning commute.

There's really unlimited potential for sea kayaking in Florida, along the Gulf of Mexico, and north along the eastern seaboard.

> ## You can simply roll up to a beach park, walk over the boardwalk, and check things out.

Blue Water Horizons

Nowhere in the continental U.S. is the lure of blue water more irresistible to kayakers than the southeastern tip of the Florida Peninsula.

From Palm Beach through Miami, 100 feet of water is within a mile and a half of the beach, a relatively easy paddle. The Gulf Stream current pushes north year-round, with water temps in the 72- to 85-degree range. Paralleling the coastline, natural ledges of anywhere from 2 feet to 20 feet occur in bands, often 30, 60, 80, 120 and 240 feet of water. Some of the exposed rock features live coral.

In the sandy areas between the ledges are countless ships, rubble piles and other artificial reefs placed by fishing clubs and county authorities over the years.

The list of fish species that pass through these waters is nearly endless, from resident groupers and snappers, to migratory sailfish and dolphin. It's a year-round fishery.

Variations on the theme are within a quick shot of other portions of the U.S. Atlantic and Gulf coastlines.

Peter Hinck, of Palm Beach, plans his ocean kayaking trips around two things: weather and structure.

"Two feet or less," is Peter's rule of thumb, speaking of the NOAA marine forecasts. Echoing countless powerboaters who've learned to take those forecasts with a grain of salt, Peter looks for the trend. "If it was three to four yesterday, and they predict two feet today, it's gonna be rough," he said.

Another weather factor to consider, especially during summer, is afternoon thunderstorms. It's best to plan an ocean trip early in the morning, to take advantage of westerly (land) breezes. Some time around noon, when the southeasterly winds resume, Peter turns for shore, using the tail wind to speed his arrival.

The structure component takes the form of the aforementioned ledges and wrecks. Spots in the 120- to 240-foot depths hold a mix of bottom and pelagic species. From a kayaker's perspective, however, those depths are problematic. The Gulf Stream is a double-edged sword, in a way; with warm water and tropical gamefish comes a never-ending current which some days may smoke along at 3 or 4 knots, faster than most guys could paddle a kayak.

Peter's answer is to use a GPS unit to set up a drift, beginning far downcurrent (south, usually) of the wreck. And rather than deploy live baits, Peter favors the thin metallic jigs.

To apply max pressure without flipping yourself in the process, keep large, deep-running fish in front of you.

"The disadvantage of the kayak, is you can't move fast," he explained. "But with jigs, you can cover the whole water column, bottom, middle and top. That gives you opportunities to fish for three species in one application. If you just had live baits at the surface, you might miss tunas in the middepth, or amberjacks down on bottom."

Greater amberjacks have been known to reach 150 pounds; tangling with such a brawler out of a kayak meets mixed reviews. Nevertheless, Peter and some of his cohorts enjoy tugging on the AJs. Little ones (to 20 pounds or so) are pretty good eating, as are the smaller but related almaco jacks and banded rudderfish.

"When fighting a big fish, keep the rod up at the front of the kayak, not out sideways; those big AJs have enough force to roll you."

Weather can turn quickly in South Florida, especially during the summer. Above and right: Trolling for dolphin, or mahi-mahi, is a pleasure using a pedal drive.

Blackfin tuna are somewhat more realistic, seldom exceeding 30 pounds, more commonly weighing in the 2- to 10-pound range.

Dolphin occasionally swim over to a kayak, checking it out as if it's just another weed patch. Peter throws a lightweight, single-hook lure, such as a DOA TerrorEyz.

"Big dolphin, you really have to tire them out before trying to land them," he advises. "Try to get a good head shot with the gaff."

Small almaco jacks, like this one caught off South Florida, make pretty good eating.

Gear and Supplies

Water, water and more water: Keeping hydrated in tropical climes is extremely important, and more so when you're a mile or more at sea.

Peter has a good system for preserving both emergency drinking water and table-grade fish catches: He brings two fish bags, a Creative Feathers and a Watertrail bag. He puts one bag inside the other, and inside that, several large Gatorade bottles which have been filled with fresh water and frozen solid.

Tackle needs are pretty basic, once natural bait is out of the picture: Two Flambeau boxes, one with metal jigs, another with soft-plastic baitfish jigs. The tackle boxes fit neatly in the pockets behind the Native Watercraft seat, alongside a handheld waterproof VHF.

Next to the seat, Peter found some ingenious uses for the Watertrail retractable Gear Keepers, clipped to a nylon ring: One he uses to hold a pair of pliers, the other a Boga Grip fish lipper.

"Palm Beach Pete" keeps lip-gripper and pliers on retractable gear-keepers. Below: speed jigs, DOA TerrorEyz and Swimming Mullet.

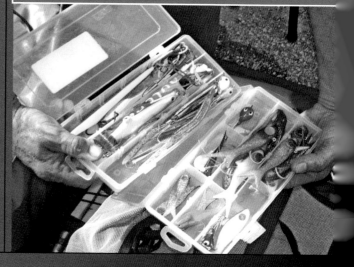

Peter puts one fish bag inside the other, and inside that, several large Gatorade bottles filled with fresh water and frozen solid.

Rob Rodriguez hauled in a 40-pound wahoo while jigging off Dania Beach, FL (Dania Pier in background). The fish struck a 5-ounce jig (bottom) in 200 feet of water. Shown at top is typical structure in this area, a coral and sponge colony on a Broward County artificial reef. Jigs such as those pictured below are ideal for these fisheries.

Tarpon Nuts

A t the northern end of Florida, where the continental shelf stretches out 40 or 50 miles, paddling to blue water is out of the question. Then again, thrill-seekers will find more than enough hair-raising seasonal action right along the beaches. We're talking tarpon. Big tarpon.

An old surfing buddy of mine from college, Shane Murray, has taken to pursuing the silver kings along New Smyrna Beach. Pursuing may not be the most accurate term, as it's more like being hauled around by tarpon.

To offer some perspective, I've landed a few little tarpon out of paddle boats, and hooked enough big ones to know that these are serious fish. In outboard boats—big boats where you can stand, or sit, or dig in a big cooler for another ice-cold drink—we've followed hooked 100-pound tarpon in and out of shipping lanes in Miami for hours; we've dogged them for miles off the Florida Keys. I've seen grown men beg for mercy, while harnessed to a stubborn tarpon.

To each his own: Shane and a surprising number of other anglers are obsessed with catching those 6-foot silver slabs that commonly outweigh the kayak. (IGFA has various awards for landing fish on tackle that's, say, one third or one-tenth the weight of the fish; wonder if they'll consider adding divisions for vessel weights?).

Anyway, you can throw all sorts of lures at beach-run tarpon, but Shane's gone to the extreme of castnetting baitfish from the kayak.

"I'll take a 6-foot net, fold it up, choke up tight, and throw it over a pod of pogies," he said, referring to the oily baitfish that gather up along Atlantic beaches in late summer. "Then I'll hoist the bait into my lap, and pour 'em into a 5-gallon bucket that's sitting in front of me. Then, I'll transfer most of the baits into a Flow-Troll bucket tethered to the kayak with a 6-foot surfboard leash, but keep a couple in the 5-gallon bucket so they're right there in case I need to re-rig."

Shane uses spinning tackle with 30- to 50-pound braided line, rigged with a double line to 60-pound-test monofilament leader and a 6/0 octopus-style J-hook.

"We slow troll the baits at paddle speed, letting them out 40 or 50 feet. When we hook up, the drag's screaming, you reach around the seat to grab the rod, and it'll straighten you out right away, pulling you with the fish."

"It's awesome, a real sleigh-ride effect. We've had a couple of 3-mile rides, and we've fought 'em for hours of the kayak.

"At the end of the fight, bring the fish alongside, snap a couple of photos. You'll want a buddy boat for sure— your companion can paddle alongside, and maybe hold the rod while you grab the leader to release the hook."

"It's best in the summer; we launch off the beach where we

find bait balls. You drive up and down looking, scouting beach crossovers, looking for pelicans diving."

There's usually a bit more swell in Smyrna than in Palm Beach; even on a calm day, there's a chance of rolling your boat on the way in. Shane's tried rod tethers, but often just uses the criss-crossing bungee tie-downs in the aft section. "When you put the rod in the rod holder, situate it so that the spinning reel handle is straight up. Pull the bungee up and over the handle to keep the rod from bouncing out."

When the pogy pods move in on North Florida beaches, ambitious anglers like Larry Stephens (here off Flagler Beach) catch bait on the spot and then hitch up for a "silver king sleigh ride."

Shane Murray, Peter Hinck, Larry Stephens—these are mild-mannered, congenial guys. Shane works in real estate; Peter for Publix supermarkets. Unlikely you'll see them belly up to a bar and launch into an epic narrative about their fishing exploits. Like many kayak anglers, they mostly enjoy doing the things they do for their own reasons. Peter does some kayak-instruction seminars, and is active on the Florida Sportsman Forum. Shane takes his little girls out on camping trips in his outboard-powered flats boat. But, when conditions line up, these guys are out there, pushing the limits, trying new stuff.

Launching is one thing, but you may end up following your boat through the surf on the way in.

Safety Issues — Palm Beach expert Peter Hinck offers hints.

The consequences of dehydration, storms and rogue fish can be mitigated to a certain extent. Boat traffic, however, represents the most clear and present danger to would-be sea kayakers on the east coast. (See Chapter 5, "Think like a Power boater.")

Peter Hinck, who fishes out of Boynton Beach, Pompano Beach and Palm Beach, Florida, recommends launching from the sand on a public beach, away from inlets. Avoid trolling right outside inlets, where transiting powerboats are likely to run over your lines. Once offshore, he says he feels somewhat safer on the edges, where dive boats frequently anchor, and powerboaters are on a constant hunt for surface debris.

A buddy system is also smart, fishing with at least one other kayaker to increase your profile on the water. "And make sure you have a float plan," Hinck added. "Write down where you'll be fishing, and give it to

When surf is rough, the kayaker may need to jump out and guide his boat safely to shore.

someone at home or the office."

In addition to the whistle or air horn which all kayakers should carry, Hinck recommends two modes of long-range communication for ocean fishing: a marine radio, and a cellular phone.

Whereas a full-foam PFD adds comfort in California and other cool regions, here in South Florida, Hinck favors the inflatable suspender-types. The manually inflatable PFD, as opposed to the ones which automatic inflate upon sensing water.

I fished with Peter on a marginal day, when we would've probably been better off in the Intracoastal Waterway. Still, it was fun watching him drag a fully-loaded, 14 ½-foot kayak (complete with wheels lashed to the back!), through the small breakers, stroke out to the reef edge, and then return to shore without missing a beat. A little gonzo, sure, but adventurous and practical, when you start to think about it.

Reading the Ocean

The Gulf of Mexico can yield some incredible catches, such as Joey Wommack's sailfish. He hooked it a quarter mile off Panama City Beach, FL, while slow-trolling a live blue runner.

Water conditions, baitfish and structure are the three main variables for locating ocean species. That goes for migratory fish such as mackerel and cobia, as well as benthic (bottom-hugging) fish including snapper and grouper.

It's important to research the habits of the species you're targeting, so that you know the right time of year to go for them, and so that you're prepared to identify the conditions that will indicate good fishing.

There are some key pre-trip planning systems I always use. One is the network of NOAA Data Buoys, stationed along and offshore the U.S. coastline. These moored buoys and fixed sensing stations (some are on drilling platforms, piers and other structures) can provide a wealth of data. Water temperature is one obvious detail. If you're expecting the mackerel to arrive along the Florida coastline, for instance, you should monitor the nearest buoy and watch for the water temp to reach the 70-degree mark. There are also satellite services, such as those accessible via the Rutgers University Coastal Ocean Observation Lab (COOL), easily found on the Internet. These show bands of water temperatures on the coastline in various shades.

Of course, wind and wave data is of vital interest to you as a kayaker. The data buoys provide immediate updates on local winds and waves. You can also check more distant buoys to ensure a long-interval ground swell isn't going to roll in and spoil your return trip onto the beach.

Hmm... I wonder where the fish are today?

If you see birds diving on bait within a comfortable paddling distance, that's a good sign. If not, check a different launch point.

Beach cameras, both single-frame and video, are a huge resource for modern kayak fishermen. You can get an instant look at what the conditions look like at the beach. Some cams also have wind and barometric pressure readings, as well as tide reports. Of course, if you're planning to head out right at sunrise, you might not have the luxury of an updated cam view, but you can see what the waves looked like the night before. Reference that image with the swells on the data buoys, the daily forecast, and the tides, and you'll have a pretty good idea of what you're dealing with.

Structure is easy to find, with a wealth of resources on various charts. Also, many state authorities print nearshore artificial reef coordinates on brochures or websites.

Last but not least, your own on-site evaluations will go a long way toward ensuring success. If you see birds diving on bait within a comfortable paddling distance, that's always a good sign. If those birds are a few miles down the beach, it may be better to move along to a different launch point.

FIshfinder/plotter combo is crucial for finding structure.

Beach cameras, such as the EVS network, are a valuable tool.

Similarly, if the water temperature or color is not to your satisfaction, you may find better conditions elsewhere.

Just as you learn discretion when it comes to safe surf launches, you'll also learn to make good calls based on fishing conditions.

The ocean is a changing medium; if a sudden upwelling moves in and pushes the fish far from the coast, no amount of fishing expertise and tackle is going to produce.

Some days, it's better to stay inshore.

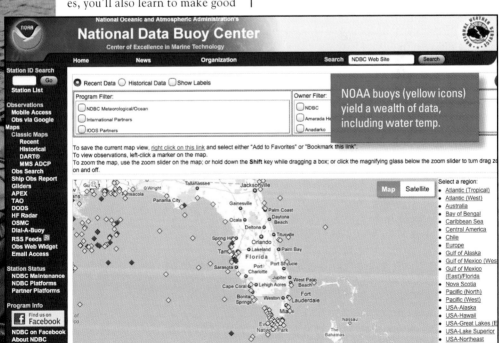

NOAA buoys (yellow icons) yield a wealth of data, including water temp.

Special Note from the Author:

Is a Powerboat Right for You?

A 23-foot center console is a good size for sailfish action.

hroughout this book I've highlighted the joys and advantages of fishing from kayaks. In many situations, kayaks open up new opportunities which may not be available to power-boaters: shallow lakes, small streams, skinny flats, remote beach launches. That the self-propelled craft also open up opportunities of boat-ownership to fishermen on a tight budget goes without saying.

But there's another topic that must be said, particularly at the close of a chapter on ocean fishing: There are places and conditions in which a powerboat really is the better choice.

Anglers who get their first taste of ocean fishing while on a kayak find it addictive. It's clear the human species has evolved an innate fascination for the ocean, the limitless possibilities. We share kinship with the dolphins and whales. Anglers who come to oceak kayaking from the other direction, scaling back from a powerboat, find it a convenient way to get out there, without paying for gas.

Both camps would surely agree that there's a limit to how far you should push it in a paddle boat. There's a dark blue line between adventure and unneeded risk. As explained in Chapter 5: Safety, risk assessment should include not only yourself, but those whose responsibility it may be to recover you in the event something goes wrong.

I've spent a lifetime around powerboats, kayaks, surfboards and every manner of ocean craft. I've owned numerous boats. And in the course of researching this book, I spent countless hours with ocean kayak fishermen on three oceans. My advice, for what it's worth:

If you enjoy routinely fishing offshore reefs for snapper and grouper, more than one mile from shore, or tackling large, acrobatic fighters such as sailfish, tarpon and dolphin, at some point in your fishing career, you're going to want a powerboat. You might not admit it, especially to kayak buds who look up to you, but inside, you'll know it.

The good news is, as a kayaker, you're uniquely qualified for powerboat ownership. You'll find yourself very comfortable on a bare-bones center console. You'll also be way ahead of the average powerboat angler, in that you've already arrived at the awareness that you just don't need a ton of stuff to catch fish in the ocean.

A basic, new 18- to 21-foot single-engine center console, with a fishfinder/GPS setup, a livewell, a VHF radio and a serviceable trailer, will set you back anywhere from $20,000 to $50,000 (sky's the limit on super premium boats). On the used

As a kayaker, you're uniquely qualified for powerboat ownership.

market, you can find a serviceable boat in this class starting around $10,000. Many are available for even less than that, but in my experience, you'll be adding fixes that will you back to the four-decimal mark. A vee-hull boat in this category is suitable for ocean work out to 10 or 12 miles—farther than you should be paddling. And, it'll get you back to port in less than an hour, if the weather turns. With the engine, you'll be able to quickly re-set a drift over a productive fishing spot in current. With an anchor and sufficient rode, you'll be able to stay put in depths out to 100 feet of water. When a big pelagic fish takes to the air, you won't have to worry about it knocking you into the water. You can stow as much food and drink as you like.

This category of powerboat generally scales in below 3,500 pounds, making it feasible to tow with a medium-size pickup or sport utility (some new boaters are shocked to learn they'll need to buy a $50,000 heavy-duty truck to pull their new cabin cruiser!). And, you'll be able to take 1 to 3 friends with you (significant others will be very pleased). The next step, class-wise, is a 23- to 25-foot vessel, which may be outfitted with twin engines, for additional range and security.

With your kayak background, you've likely developed a fondness for tinkering. If the powerboat hull is in decent shape (deck and transom are solid) and the engine is in good condition, you'll likely be able to fix cosmetic, electrical and rigging issues. Have a mechanic inspect the engine, and you do a little Web searching to find out about potential issues with the particular model year you're looking at. A water-test is always a good idea.

One of my own first boats was a used 17-foot Hydra-Sports center console with a 140-horsepower Evinrude. I bought it for $7,000 cash when I lived in Miami, fished it hard for 4 years, caught

Bay boat with high horse-power engine, for when you need to cover lots of miles.

innumerable sailfish, kings, wahoo, tarpon, dolphin, snappers, trout. During my ownership, I sold the trailer for a few hundred dollars, kept the boat in a marina, did most of the maintenance myself, added a leaning post and livewell. When I moved out of town, I sold the boat for a little over $4,000, after deducting for some steering and engine work I knew she needed. I figured the annual cost of boat ownership, including maintenance, fuel, insurance, storage and depreciation, came to around $3,000. That's about the cost of some kayaks, once you trick them out and ac-

count for transport racks and other necessities.

Estimates like this are just what they are—estimates. The main point is, if you can find a decent little boat, store it at home (I paid marina fees), and get buddies to kick in for fuel and maintenance, you might find you aren't spending a whole lot more than you are on your kayak adventures.

You'll be safer and more comfortable in the open ocean, and you'll likely find a balanced outlook that will make you appreciate the kayak days even more. Want to paddle off the beach for an hour or two on a calm day? Take the kayak. Want to spend 8 hours working the reefs for snapper? Take the powerboat.

You might even take both, lashing the kayak inside your powerboat for a long-range trip! SB

CHAPTER 14

Friends Near and Far

Kayak anglers are an interesting sort. They're usually fishing alone, by choice, in a one-man boat. At the same time, they're among the most social of fishing groups. In future decades, a sociologist might make sense out of this apparent contradiction, but for now we take it as a given: Where there's one kayak, there'll soon be another. And they won't be shouting at each other, they'll be waving! The Internet finds kayakers sharing the kinds of rigging and fishing secrets that past generations would've guarded from all but the most trusted friends. Tournaments tend to be social events, without the stress of big-money jackpots. Are these guys crazy? Maybe, but if so, it's a good kind of crazy. Will the laid-back attitude prevail? We hope so!

In future decades, a sociologist might make sense out of the apparent contradiction. Are these guys crazy? Maybe so, but it's a good kind of crazy.

Benton Parrott, left, is surely thinking of the kayak he won at a GCKFA tourney in Pensacola. Top: Jose Chavez at Hobie World Championship.

Calling all Kayakers

Fishing alone, in a group: Events like this Kayak Fishing Radio "Boondoggle" bring anglers together.

Chuck Levi, featured with a fine seatrout in Chapter 10, is a 32-year-old resident of Titusville, Florida, and a retired deputy sheriff. He does some part time guiding, and works with area tackle shops and outfitters.

Among his recent projects is a stint as a Monday night host on Kayak Fishing Radio, a blogtalkradio.com feature that's interesting and informative.

With a co-host and occasional guests, Chuck discusses kayak gear, fishing tactics, and upcoming events. One big event in February 2011 was a "Boondoggle" held down in Chokoloskee. Primed by the radio broadcasts and chatroom acquaintances, the Boondoggle—like others held by KFR—drew fishermen from as far away as New York.

"Chip Gibson started the first show in Atlanta, GA, two years ago," said Chuck. "It was a round-table discussion format where guys get together and talk about their time on the water, ask questions of one another."

This spawned a second show, and now there are five shows, one every night of the work week, starting at 8 p.m.

Hosts from Virginia Beach, Georgia, California, and Florida bring together a diverse audience, from freshwater paddlers to open-sea warriors.

There's always something new to learn. Check out the gallery of kayaks gathered below.

Cash, Prizes, and Sporting Competition

The Inshore Fishing Association (IFA) got its start in skiff and bayboat competition for redfish catches. Soon, it also branched into a Kayak Fishing Tour, with events from Texas to the Carolinas.

The 2011 season attracted anglers from around the southeastern United States, including Justin Carter, of Mt. Pleasant, South Carolina. It also attracted big-name sponsors, including Hobie Cat.

The IFA Kayak events are all-release, with scoring based on aggregate inches for redfish and seatrout, one of each per day. At the two-day 2011 IFA Championship in Chalmette, Louisiana, Carter caught two redfish and two speckled trout measuring a combined 105 inches. He mostly fished around the Hopedale sector of the giant, rich Mississippi River delta, casting hard plugs. That was in the middle of November, when weather can be dicey.

"The first day was nice and calm. I caught 25 reds in deep water and lots of small trout," Carter said. "The second day the wind picked up and the fishing was spotty, but overall the tournament was great."

Among the prizes Carter took back to South Carolina included a Hobie Mirage Pro-Angler and $1,000 cash for the IFA Angler of the Year award. Now, that's nothing compared to the loot picked up by top earners on the freshwater bass powerboat fishing circuits, but it's certainly encouraging. Also consider: Entry fee per IFA Kayak event was $75, and the scoring system highlighted sportsmanlike conduct. Each entrant fishes alone, and photographs his own catches, on a special measuring device, with a date token. Other rules include artificial lures only, and no trolling.

All around the U.S., kayakers are finding countless local, unaffiliated kayak fishing tournaments using a similar format. Some have gear regulations, such as maximum length for wading tethers, and location restrictions, as within a certain radius of the weigh-in. A common thread that runs through all: No motors may be used.

Prowess with artificial lures on a variety of waters (Louisiana, below) propelled South Carolina kayaker Justin Carter to the top of the IFA ranks in 2011.

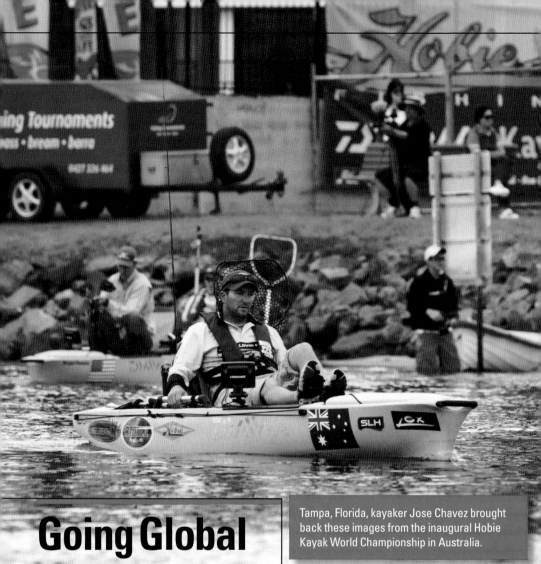

Going Global

Tampa, Florida, kayaker Jose Chavez brought back these images from the inaugural Hobie Kayak World Championship in Australia.

Loading up and heading down the coast is one thing. Imagine traveling halfway around the world to meet fellow kayak anglers. In our digitally connected world, making friends overseas is a snap.

Growing enthusiasm for competition also brings anglers of different nationalities to common waters, where fishing tactics and lifestyles are shared.

In the summer of 2011, Hobie Cat held its first ever World Championship. The event was put on in conjunction with the final event in the Australian kayak fishing circuit. The destination was Port Macquarie, on the east coast of Australia.

A Florida kayaker born in Guatemala, Jose Chavez is in many ways the epitome of the 21st-century outdoorsman. A microbiology consultant

living in the Tampa Bay area, Chavez is a member of the HardCore Kayak Anglers club. He says he "tries" to fish at least twice a week, but his modesty belies a lifelong commitment to the sport.

After strong finishes in U.S. regional events, Chavez was picked to fish the Hobie Championship.

"Preparing for the trip, I didn't really know what to expect," he said, just days after returning from Australia. "I did some research online; the fish we targeted was yellowfin bream, a small saltwater fish that gets up to maybe 8 or 9 pounds. I knew we'd be fishing strong current, and deep structure, so I brought some lures I have confidence in: itty bitty plastic shrimp, other jigs.

"People I met there were super nice, super friendly—guys would never hesitate to say,

this is working, or this is not, or here's some extra jigheads.

"Australia has a very lively kayak fishing circuit—it reminded me more of how the bass fishing world is in the U.S., with sponsorships and endorsements.

"The two rivers we fished over three days were the Camden and Hastings, beautiful rivers with big trees, mountains covered with heavy vegetation."

Hobie provided the kayaks, Pro Angler models which Chavez was familiar with from Florida waters. He said the MirageDrive pedal propulsion was especially useful for holding in the current over deep ledges in 20 feet of water.

"It was mostly vertical fishing; the majority of fish I caught were from these oyster farming racks. I'd set up downcurrent, hold in the current, and run the baits through the structure—vertical jigs and small vibrating crankbaits."

"Yellowfin bream are leader-shy, and leader diameter made a huge difference—using 4-pound test, you'd get bites, then bump it up to 6-pound, and the bites diminished."

"The Australian kayak circuit reminded me of the U.S. bass fishing world, with sponsorships and endorsements."

"I moved from Guatemala to the U.S. when I was 14 or 15. We always fished offshore in Guatemala, but I had no access to a boat in Florida, so I started wade fishing and pier fishing. One day, as I was wading a half-mile to a spot, a guy in a kayak flew by me, hit my spot, caught a fish, and kept going. I said to myself, 'I'm doing this!'"

"The Hard Core Kayak club is a really friendly club. People bring their families. We have monthly events which bring some of our 500 members. On Saturdays, we might fish and get off the water between 10 and noon and then have a big cookout."

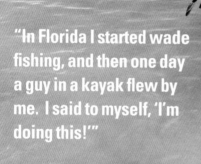

"In Florida I started wade fishing, and then one day a guy in a kayak flew by me. I said to myself, 'I'm doing this!'"

Florida Panhandle

Kayaking is growing fast along Florida's westernmost coastline, that narrow band of piney woods and sugar-white sand between Port St. Joe and the Alabama state line.

Here, deep, blue water runs close to shore. There are wrecks and reefs in 60 feet of water within a mile of shore, loaded up with red snapper, kingfish and grouper. The big bays, Pensacola, Choctawhatchee, West and St. Joe, are clear water with lush seagrass, ideal habitat for spotted seatrout and red drum. Rivers and streams flowing into the bays are slow-moving and rich with life. There are native striped bass populations in some parts, as well as largemouth bass, big redear sunfish, and unusual river critters such as flathead catfish and sturgeon.

The people here are friendly and genuine, many of them family members of military servicemen and women at the nearby Air Force and Naval bases.

Ferd Salomon is president of the Gulf Coast Kayak Fishing Association, a 100-plus-member club based in Pensacola, Florida. He's a retired Naval pilot, currently a real estate broker.

"We have a lot of guys who fish the bays, rivers and bayous, for reds, trout, flounder, small sharks," said Salomon. "And some parts of the bay get really deep—you can catch red snapper and grouper in the bay. There's also an active group of kayakers who fish offshore, for king mackerel, Spanish mackerel. We've even had guys pull in dolphin, and in the summer of 2011, sailfish came in real close. Blackfin tuna, too. Some of the hardcore guys will go out 5 or 6 miles to bottom numbers."

Salomon said the Association holds regular clinics in the Pensacola area. Members will bring their rigged-out kayakers, and set them up for people to see. It's usually a low-key program, just guys hanging out, talking fishing.

The Kayak Fishing Association puts on an annual tournament at Shoreline Park in Gulf Breeze, a little town between Pensacola and the beach. National and local sponsors chip in for prizes, including Hooters, Hobie, Hot Spots Bait and Tackle, Sandy Sansing Nissan, and Academy Sports. It's held each year in late April, a time of year when migratory fish arrive and local bays are in prime condition. Local fishermen are usually chomping at the bit to get out, too, after the typically cool and breezy winters.

In 2012, the tournament was held in honor of LCpl Travis Nelson, USMC, "an avid kayak fisherman and Pace High grad, who was killed in Afghanistan in August 2011," said Salomon. "We will contribute a portion of the proceeds of the tournament to the LCpl Travis Nelson Scholarship Fund. His parents, Scott and Beckie, have set up the fund to award two seniors from the ROTC programs in Santa Rosa and Escambia County $500 to $1,000 toward their college tuition. We thought that this would be a great way to raise monies because of Travis' love for saltwater fishing. Our tournament shirt has a camouflage theme to it with Travis in mind."

The Future: Kids and Kayaks

A calm, protected lake is the place for those first strokes. Offer encouragement, and perhaps enlist another child to watch and learn.

First things first: Able to swim without help? Check. Can name the different parts of a kayak and a paddle? Check, check.

Has been tossed from a kayak, into a swimming pool—or calm, clean bay—wearing a life vest, and required to swim a short distance, either to shore or back to the kayak?

You've probably thought about the easy stuff. A comfy life vest. Water bottle close by, some favorite snacks. But introducing a youngster to the paddling lifestyle should be more involved than that.

Safety is priority number one. In open water, don't expect to rely on your own life-saving skills to keep your child afloat. If you're incapacitated, your kid must be able to fend for himself. He must be able to keep his head above water and regain hold of the kayak. He must be able

> **Don't start off mixing kayaking with fishing. Teach a child about fishing gear in a safe, comfortable spot on shore.**

to make noise. And he must be able to maintain some composure until help arrives.

As time goes on, your mutual confidence will exponentially increase the satisfaction level of your fishing trips.

Start early, and go easy. It may take several years before your child is ready to join you on longer trips. Find a swimming pool or protected inshore water body to introduce a youngster to the kayak and life jacket.

Don't start off mixing kayaking with fishing. Teach your child about fishing gear in a safe, comfortable spot onshore. A fishing pier, a backyard lake, a stable powerboat: These are better places to master the basics of fishing.

Before you try putting the fishing into the kayak, I'd recommend spending one or two summers on the following two kinds of trips.

The Pool

In a comfortable, familiar swimming pool, the learning process practically takes care of itself. Let it be fun. The child might want to make a game of it; if so, play along!

Paddle your kayak away from the side. At first, your child will enjoy swimming out to the kayak, and then swimming back to shore to be with Mama or another swimming adult (this person is a critical part of your team).

Next, she'll likely want to swim out, grab the side of the kayak, and try to drag you back to shore with her.

Put her in your lap, and let her make some strokes. Odds are good, she'll soon want to flop out of the kayak and swim to shore. Encourage this!

Now, try having her flop out

and you pull her back into the kayak.

Last but not least, put the two of you in the water, and then retake the kayak. It's not easy, but it's a critical rite of passage. You'll probably need to get in first.

If the two of you can perform these maneuvers and laugh about it, you're ready for some open water.

1) In a safe environment, with a good swimmer as your partner, practice falling out together.

2) A potential fishing-mate must be capable of holding onto the kayak alone. This is critical.

3) Now, you re-enter the kayak (see Chapter 5)...

4) ...and then pull your partner to safety.

5) If you can do this, you're ready for open water together.

On the Bay or Lake

Early trips on the kayak, let the child sit with you for easy trips of very short duration, close to home: Around a backyard lake, one lap. To a sandbar on a coastal lagoon. Little trips you take for granted can be the stuff of dreams for a kid. Imagine finding clear water, smooth sand, seagrass beds close enough to reach with a long cast. On low tide, you might disembark and walk a sandbar, looking for whelks and sea urchins, tiny fish trapped in tide pools. As your child gains confidence, you might wade-fish while towing him or her behind you.

Most important: The open water trips should be no longer than an hour or two. You must suspend your own ambitions and instead think of your new friend. Their comfort and satisfaction are vital to forging a future relationship. Telling a hungry, sunweary child to be still and wait while Daddy tries for another fish is not a productive way to introduce them to kayak fishing. Paddle shoreward for a seashell hunt. Duck into some shade for a few minutes. Stimulate your child's imagination: The two of you are Indians, paddling for an unexplored world. You won't be far off the mark.

Malibu offers a range of family boats, from small single Mini-X, above, to tandem models, middle.

Forward Gator Hatch has a molded seat area for one child, while another "stows away" in the tankwell. Go for a short paddle, then take a break on shore.

Dear Department of Parks and Recreation:

More Launches Like This!

Shown here is a very handy paddle-craft launch lane at a public boat ramp in Martin County, Florida. Where it's not possible or practical to beach the kayak, you may have to use a nearby dock. Which of course presents a few problems—one being, the kayak tends to slide out and away from you when you get in or out. This design here solves that problem and more. Stemming off from the main dock, out of sight beneath the kayak, is a metal cradle. It holds the timber on the outside, which keeps the boat close to the dock. The decking has been lowered, and rails added, to ease access to and from the cockpit. This is especially important for sit-inside style kayaks, such as the inflatable model shown here.

Retrofitting docks for safe and convenient paddle craft access would be a good project for local fishing clubs. Contact your local department of parks and recreation, or perhaps your fish and game department. SB

> ## Retrofitting docks for paddle craft access would be a good project for local clubs.

Handy kayak and canoe lane on a small river in Southeast Florida.

Simply paddle into the lane. . .

. . . unload some of your gear. . .

. . . and now step out of the kayak, without fear of it slipping out from under you.

CHAPTER 15

Standup Paddleboards

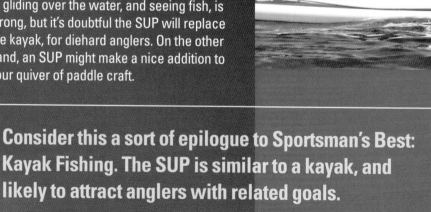

If you really want to get up out of your seat, and don't mind falling down now and then, try a standup paddleboard, or SUP. Consider this is a sort of epilogue to Sportsman's Best: Kayak Fishing—the SUP is similar to a kayak, and likely to attract anglers with similar goals. Coastal anglers in recent years have explored the fishing possibilities with these craft, which entered the paddle world by way of the surfing world. The SUP is basically like a giant surfboard, but with enough flotation to keep the paddler on top while at rest. Some of them are in fact designed to ride waves, though the more practical fishing models are not. The thrill of gliding over the water, and seeing fish, is strong, but it's doubtful the SUP will replace the kayak, for diehard anglers. On the other hand, an SUP might make a nice addition to your quiver of paddle craft.

Consider this a sort of epilogue to Sportsman's Best: Kayak Fishing. The SUP is similar to a kayak, and likely to attract anglers with related goals.

Builders of the BOTE board are exploring options for leaning-posts and deck-mount storage.

Built to Glide

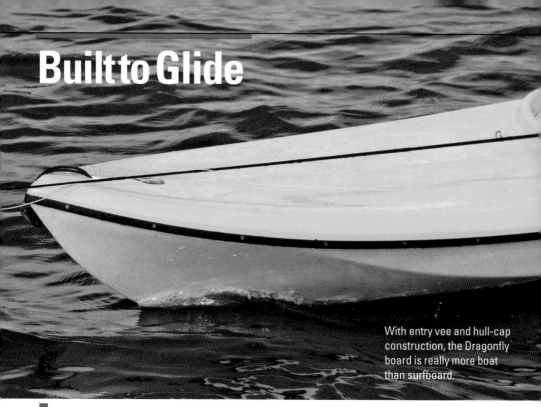

With entry vee and hull-cap construction, the Dragonfly board is really more boat than surfboard.

If you plan to do a lot of sight-fishing, or simply don't enjoy sitting for long periods, a standup paddleboard (SUP) or hybrid might be in your future. The added elevation opens up a better angle of vision into the water. Plus, the walk-on-the-water thrill is undeniable.

That said, you really should test one of these vessels in mixed conditions before buying. Bucking a head wind across a mile-wide bay, for example, is very difficult when you're standing. The wind pushes against you like a sail.

On the other hand, in calm water, you can cover impressive distances from a SUP. And, you can tap your entire body—legs, hips, abdomen, back, shoulders, arms—to make very efficient paddle strokes. Once you get a feel for the system, you'll likely notice you're moving faster than you would in a traditional kayak—until you face the wind. At that point, you'll wish you were lower to the water.

There are kayaks built to accommodate standup fishing, too. The Hobie ProAngler, for instance, may be propelled with a pushpole in the same manner as a flats skiff. Outrigger-float accessories may also be added to kayaks and canoes.

But there's something liberating about stroking a SUP across a quiet pond or saltwater flat. Many hardcore fishermen add one of these vessels to their collection simply for the enjoyment factor, if nothing else.

Most of the surfing-style SUPs consist of fiberglass laminated over shaped polystyrene or polyurethane foam. They aren't typically designed to accommodate gear or heavy loads, and while they may be configured for exceptional maneuverability, there are limitations to what can be done.

Hull-and-cap construction, as in the Dragonfly Board, seems to open up more possibilities for fishing amenities. The Dragonfly is built much like a fiberglass flats boat: In two parts, the hull (bottom) and the deck (top). The pieces are shoe-boxed together and sealed with adhesive, with a rubrail covering the cap. Hull repair is treated exactly as with a fiberglass boat—gelcoat dings may be patched, glass mat added to cover holes.

Inside, the board is hollow, except for cross-members every 7 inches. The cross-members,

> ## You can cover impressive distances, tapping your entire body for efficient paddle strokes.

Surfing-style SUPs aren't typically designed to carry gear or heavy loads.

Alabama's Jimbo Meador enjoys fly casting on the Dragonfly Board.

explains Mark Castlow, are Innegra: "Same material as in the bumpers of cars, a beaded polypropylene, with a high degree of memory. It offers some give to the surface." SeaDeck non-skid foam is also applied to the deck surface, making this truly a barefoot boat.

The 13-foot board (a 10-footer is offered, as well) weighs in the mid 40-pound range, which is lighter than a rotomolded poly kayak of similar proportions. The bow has a slight vee to it, and the rails (sides) are built up forward to shed water while paddling. The bottom is mostly flat.

Partnering with Castlow in the design of the Dragonfly was Jimbo Meador, of Alabama. Meador helped integrate some subtle but clever design elements, including a toe rail which starts at about one-third of the way forward and runs aft.

"One of the drawbacks to a surfing-style board

Mark Castlow shoulders the 40-pound Dragonfly 13. Closeup of tail fin, or skeg, right.

is, the water can come over the deck, and if you've stripped the fly line on there, it'll wash your line off. These have little rails that contain the fly line, plus it keeps the deck dry, too."

Testing a Dragonfly 13, I found the rail also helped keep my waterproof backpack and camera box from slipping over.

I've paddled a number of SUPs over the years, but the Dragonfly felt different. When I hooked a nice snook off a mangrove point, I found I had

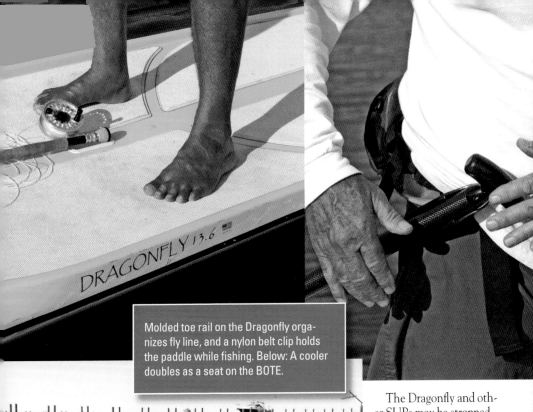

Molded toe rail on the Dragonfly organizes fly line, and a nylon belt clip holds the paddle while fishing. Below: A cooler doubles as a seat on the BOTE.

The Dragonfly and other SUPs may be strapped to a roofrack for transport. The single fin, or skeg, is fiberglass. For access to super skinny water (traditionally a problem for surf-style SUPs, with their long stabilizing fin), the Dragonfly designers are working on a shallow-water fin, with greater surface area longitudinally, and less vertical draft.

Don't expect the bigger, skiff-style paddleboards to perform like surfing SUPs. These boats are designed for flat water, perhaps a light chop at most. If you wish to mix things up with some backwater fishing and occasional free-surfing on the ocean rollers, look for a more traditional SUP, such as the BOTE board. Also, local surfboard shapers in coastal areas have picked up on the demand for what's essentially a scaled-up version of a surfing longboard. Many of these craftsmen can custom-build a standup paddle board that should perform to your specifications and body size.

enough stability to sort of back paddle away from cover while holding the fishing rod. And, I was able to kneel down to release the fish.

These are the kinds of movements that you'd want to attempt before buying a SUP, or loading up valuable gear to join a buddy.

Meador mostly fly-fishes, and said he'll bring a fanny pack with some flies and leader material. To the belt, he attaches a swiveling paddle clip, which holds the long paddle when the time comes to cast.

Armand Croteau paddles one of his SIK Boardz on the Caloosahatchee River in Fort Myers, Florida. He designed the board to accommodate a swivel seat, flush-mount rod holders, as well as integrated dry storage.

Florida's Indian River Lagoon

Round Island Park, where we previewed the Dragonfly SUP, is one of several public access points along the famous Indian River Lagoon in east central Florida. This park, on Hutchinson Island south of Vero Beach, has restrooms, paved boat ramps, and an unimproved launch for paddle craft.

Kayaks and SUPs are ideal for the Lagoon, which runs almost 150 miles from Hobe Sound, in Martin County, to Ponce Inlet, in Volusia County. The Lagoon is a narrow waterway, 2 miles across at the widest point, and in most stretches less than a mile. Mangrove islands and emergent shoals dot the Lagoon, offering plenty of places to fish in calm water. If the wind is hard out of the east, fishing the eastern side of the Lagoon will provide optimal conditions. In a west wind, head for the west side. The water is mostly 2 to 6 feet deep.

The main species to target are spotted seatrout, redfish and, in the southern sectors of the Lagoon, snook. Casting topwater plugs or soft-plastic jerkbaits is a good way to locate fish, especially in low light or adjacent to points, dropoffs and other fish-holding features. With adequate sunlight, sight-fishing for redfish is an exciting and very productive method, and that's going to require standing, either in a wide-body kayak, one with stabilizers, or on a SUP. Flycasting with a streamer or crab fly is one of the best ways to catch reds that are tailing or cruising the flats. For spinning tackle, try soft-plastic shrimp, paddle-tails, jerkbaits, or the ace-in-the-hole: a live shrimp or a small chunk of fresh-cut mullet. Seatrout and snook will also oblige the sight-fisherman, but they tend to be much spookier than the reds. For these two wary ambush-feeders, it's better to make long search casts into likely lies.

Tidal flow is minimal throughout most of the Lagoon, with the exception of areas close to inlets. The main channels of ocean inlets, including Ponce, Sebastian, Fort Pierce and St. Lucie, should be avoided by paddle craft, as there's a twin risk of being overwhelmed by the current or collision with powerboat.

Water and air temperatures are mild in this region, and it's not uncommon to be paddling in midwinter wearing surf shorts and a long-sleeve UV shirt. Occasional bouts of strong winds and icy temps following cold fronts are usually unproductive for fishing, but when the wind abates, sight-fishing can be outstanding.

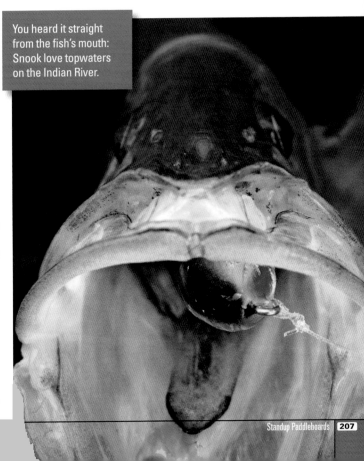

You heard it straight from the fish's mouth: Snook love topwaters on the Indian River.

SUP Hybrids

Standup paddleboards entered fishing circles by way of the surfing culture. Today they're meeting similar designs coming from the other direction—fishing skiffs and kayaks.

There are hybrid-style SUPs which may be equipped with seats from which to paddle, even molded compartments to hold coolers and other gear.

A Sarasota, Florida, builder introduced the XFish SUF/SUP vessel. At 85 pounds, for most anglers it's going to require a second person to help launch, and may be best hauled on trailer. But for anglers who plan to mix standup fishing with multiple propulsion options, this class of craft is worth investigating. In addition to the long standup paddle, the XFish may be propelled by a twin-blade kayak stroke or a transom-mounted 12-volt electric motor.

Hybrid style standup platform built in Florida: The XFish SUF/SUP.

Special Safety Concerns

With any of these vessels, safety should be of the utmost concern. It almost goes without saying that falling overboard is a distinct likelihood, and the "footprint" of these vessels makes them less visible to powerboaters.

Fine redfish caught from a SUP and self-documented by Sam Root.

The U.S. Coast Guard classifies paddleboards as vessels, and therefore the safety requirements are the same as for kayaks: an approved PFD must be on board (and worn by passengers 12 or under, in many states), sound-producing device (whistle) and visual distress/navigation signal (waterproof flashlight as a minimum). The only places the safety requirements are not enforced are within designated swimming areas and the surf zone. The former is generally unfavorable for fishing, while the latter is precisely the kind of place most anglers really ought to be wearing a PFD.

In many states, including Florida, a motor-propelled hybrid boat, no matter what size, would need to be registered.

As with kayaks, it's wise to seek instruction from a veteran paddler. And definitely practice recovering after a fall. If you find you are unable to quickly re-board an SUP in open water, consider a different vessel and/or limit your excursions to shallow water. Keep it simple: Master the system before you take your fishing tackle. SB

You will need a PFD for your SUP, and one with plenty of pockets, like this NRS model, is a good option.

CHAPTER 16

Final Notes and Resources

Our kayak fishing journey has only just begun. Investing in a kayak, and learning to fish it well under different conditions, is a good start. So is making connections with fellow anglers. But there is so much more to learn. In this final chapter, we tackle what might be termed "loose ends." Not that the subjects wouldn't fit elsewhere, but rather these topics lead naturally to ongoing pursuits: Testing your gear; learning to care for your body; setting records. Also, we include contact information for a wealth of resources, from shops to associations, for any unanswered question you may have from the other 15 chapters of this resource book.

We tackle ongoing pursuits: testing your gear; learning to care for your body; setting records. Also, we include contacts for a wealth of resources.

Weighing a potential record or releasing for another day? Soft rubber mesh keeps a trout's slime coat intact. Frabill Pro-Formance net from Settles Bridge Supply House in North Carolina.

Test Your Gear, Your Body

There's a wealth of information on the Internet, and in magazines and books like this.

Still, there's no substitute for personal experience, especially when it comes to topics that may involve life or death situations. Here's a good example.

It's an obvious question for any boater: Will this thing sink? Well, one of the great things about kayaks is, you can actually find out, without worrying about damage to mechanical or electrical systems. Powerboaters do everything possible to ensure their vessels don't sink, then lie awake wondering, what happens if? Kayakers can actually get out of bed and find out!

Maybe you'll wander around in Internet chat rooms trying to determine whether a particular model is "unsinkable," or you might stumble into discussions of various means of adding flotation. Long-range sea kayakers in sit-inside vessels are justifiably attuned to these lines of reasoning, due in equal parts to the enclosed design of the boat (holding water) as well as the relative distance from help.

One dark and stormy night (seriously!), I said what the heck, let's figure it out. If you're going to test something this important, don't do it on a bright, sunny day. Do it when it would really count, but do it in a controlled environment.

I took my 9-foot rotomolded sit-on-top, dropped it in a swimming pool, opened the main hatch, and ran a garden hose right into the hull. What manner of catastrophe this would resemble, and whether I'd survive the initial blow, was beside the point; I wanted to know. In a few minutes, the good ship gradually settled until the water level was even with the seat. But she didn't sink. I pulled the plug, making sure there were no trapped

Ever lie awake wondering whether your boat could sink? Why not find out? When it comes to safety subjects, trust but verify.

air pockets. Still, she floated. I got into the pool, and pushed the kayak under water. Down she went, slowly, but when I let go, she came back.

Now, I began adding foam pool noodles to the hull compartment, one on each side. I'd read about this, but like everything I read, I wanted to check it firsthand. The kayak floated a bit higher, but I could still push her under. I kept stuffing floats of all size and description into the boat: 6 noodles, three kickboards, a foam football, a water wing, a child's inflatable floatie. No matter how much junk I crammed into the boat, she never returned to a condition in which paddling would be feasible. Yes, the flotation bought a little extra visibility in the event of a search-and-rescue operation, but not enough to support my body above water.

The good news, for what it's worth, is my kayak is unsinkable. With extra flotation, she floats a little better, but not enough to get anywhere. With an emergency bilge pump, I could pump her out and perhaps get going again. The bad news

is, we're not going anywhere fast. Unless I'm close to shore, I'm in a survival situation, awaiting help.

Comparing PFD vs. no PFD in a swamped boat, it was an easy conclusion: A PFD vest provided far more buoyancy than the flooded kayak, even with all the floaties inside it. If I didn't have a jacket, I would've been in a bigger fix.

Really In Hot Water Now... Don't I Wish!

While I was busy testing my kayak, I was testing something else: My own body.

On that dark and stormy night, I'll admit that I had neglected to properly tighten the straps on my PFD; it rode up to my ears when I first jumped in. That lesson was justification enough for the late-night escapade.

But something else crept in, as I was fiddling around at 2 a.m. with my vest and ridiculous array of pool toys: Even in an 80-degree pool, in 70-degree air, I was getting cold, fast. Maybe it was the darkness, or the wind, or the absurd hour. I don't know. But within 30 minutes, I was uncomfortable. The PFD preserved some core warmth, much better than without one, but still the specter of hypothermia entered the picture: shivering, teeth chattering.

Had I filed a float plan, and been equipped with signaling equipment (whistle, light, flares, long-range communications described in Chapter 5), I could've stayed with the swamped kayak, and whatever noodles or other gear I opted to stash in her, until help arrived.

But how long could I have stayed alive?

After an hour, I called it quits and went inside the house to warm up. Not only did I come away with a mythbusting moment (noodles: can't hurt), I arrived at a more humble assessment of my own tolerance for discomfort.

Psychologists call this miscalculated fear, like how someone may be afraid of flying in an airplane, and yet blithely unaware of the vastly greater risks of driving a car. You think it's a sinking boat, or drowning, that'll do you in, when it's something more insidious, loss of body heat.

But don't trust me. Try it yourself. Get out of your cozy bed and go sink your kayak, then think long and hard about your safety gear and your plans.

I actually sleep better knowing there are limits to where I can go in my kayak.

Added flotation, top, helped the flooded kayak float a little higher, but not enough to keep the author out of cold water. He needs a PFD, float plan and distress signals.

Sample Float Plan

One of the most important things you should do as a kayaker is file a float plan with a trusted source who'll be onshore and close to a phone for the duration of your trip. That might be a spouse or good friend, or a co-worker.

Not only should you provide the place and time of your departure and expected return, but sufficient information to help rescuers locate you in the event something goes wrong. And write it down!

Here is a basic outline which you may wish to copy. Or, make your own float plan, adding any pertinent data, for instance if you or another kayaker has a chronic medical issue.

Float Plan

Date: _____   Time of Departure: _____

Point of Departure: _____

Intended Destination(s): _____

Point of Return: _____

Expected Time of Return: _____

Number of Vessels and Persons: _____

Kayak Model(s) and Color: _____

Communications: _____

         VHF Frequency: _____

         Cellular Phone: _____

Even a quick trip to a shoreline red-fish flat should begin with notifying someone where you'll be.

Fishing Log

Now that you've become acquainted with kayak fishing tactics, and learned to document trip plans for safety (facing page), it's time to chronicle your fishing trips for your own personal benefit.

Social media and the proliferation of media in general provide countless avenues to obtain fishing reports. New anglers, in particular, are quick to "bite" on shared tidbits of information. But after a time, you may find it more rewarding to rely on your own knowledge. There's a real thread of self-sufficiency at the root of kayak fishing— you're using your own energy to get to the fish. Why not use your own mental energy?

To the right is an example of a fishing log. You might use these categories to begin your own log, either on the computer, or perhaps in an old-school spiral notebook. Digital options are limitless; the accompanying image shows a Google Maps entry by a Florida kayak fisherman.

Remember that it's just as important to log poor fishing days as it is successful ones (one of the big drawbacks to social media is that it selects only for the good news). You'll find it remarkable what you can learn merely from observing fish and conditions, even when they aren't lining up the way you wish.

Also, the categories below may be mixed, for instance you might note the depth at which you observed forage fish, and later compare it to the sunlight on different days.

Date: _____ **Time:** _____

Location(s) fished: _____

Weather conditions: _____

Moon phase: _____

Tide (or current): _____

Gamefish species observed (and est. number): _____

Forage species observed: _____

Fish landed: _____

Productive depth: _____

Structure: _____

Lures or bait used: _____

Other anglers present: _____

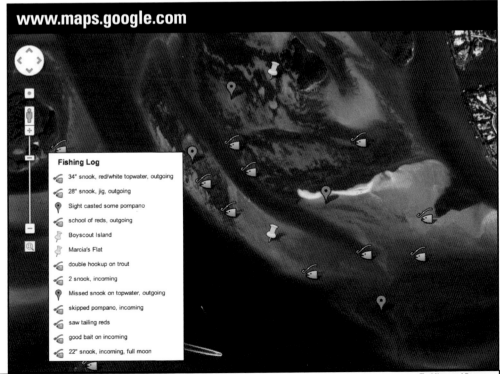

www.maps.google.com

Fishing Log

- 34" snook, red/white topwater, outgoing
- 28" snook, jig, outgoing
- Sight casted some pompano
- school of reds, outgoing
- Boyscout Island
- Marcia's Flat
- double hookup on trout
- 2 snook, incoming
- Missed snook on topwater, outgoing
- skipped pompano, incoming
- saw tailing reds
- good bait on incoming
- 22" snook, incoming, full moon

Healthy Paddling

In the first chapter, on selecting kayaks, and at various intervals in this book, we've reinforced the benefits of learning proper technique from certified instructors. That goes for basic flatwater paddling, sea kayaking and moving water.

Your future in kayaking should not be merely devoted to getting from point A to point B, but maintaining a pain-free, satisfying hobby.

Kayakers at each end of the spectrum are vulnerable to aches and pains.

We know about wearing our PFDs to stay afloat, but in the interest of helping all of us keep our bodies in tiptop shape, I interviewed two medical professionals intimately involved with kayaking. By design, I selected experts at different ends of the spectrum: Michael Rosenberg is a physical therapist and rehabilitation specialist for the USA Canoe/Kayak Team; Debra Kettler is a recreational sea kayaking coach with a background in chiropractic medicine. One works with elite-level athletes (well, Debra has done that, too!), the other provides instruction to interested members of the public in San Diego, California.

The fact is, kayakers at each end of the spectrum are vulnerable to aches and pain, albeit for somewhat different reasons. Let's have a look.

New Kayakers

Debra Kettler is uniquely qualified to be a kayaking instructor: Not only is she a certified BCU-UKCC Level 2 coach (www.Aqua-Adventures.com), she is a retired chiropractor. She knows how to avoid injuries, and knows the consequences of improper posture and technique.

Common overuse injuries among recreational kayakers involve the shoulder, elbow and various muscles of the arms, said Kettler. Macho angler and surfer-types with "beach muscles" are espe-

I asked for advice on the

cially vulnerable—we tend to push too hard.

"Someone not trained in kayaking, they're not thinking, 'What's the most efficient method to propel this kayak?'" Kettler said. "They're usually powering and using their upper body strength."

"Right," I replied, "guys like me, we're thinking about getting out there to the fish, fast!"

I asked Kettler for some basic advice on optimizing the paddle stroke. These were things I knew I needed to hear:

• First, maintain an upright, forward posture, sitting tall in your seat, and not relying on your back band for support.

Fishermen can learn a great deal from instructors like Debra Kettler, shown here. Feeling aches? Take your mind off casting and focus on paddling.

basic stroke. These were things I knew I needed to hear.

• The rotation in your body, for a proper stroke, should begin at the hips—not just in the arms.

• When you reach to make the catch—paddle blade in the water at your toes—your chest should be facing the opposite direction. For instance, if you're paddling on the left side, your chest should face to the right, which moves the left shoulder and hip farther forward than the right shoulder and hip, to get the farthest reach. As you power through the stroke, your chest rotates to the opposite side, hips and shoulder moving, and have the blade come out by the time your hand reaches your hip.

• An efficient stroke makes use of the entire body. As the blade goes into the water, push through with your foot, which allows your knee and hip to rotate back, and your leg to straighten as you come through with the stroke, driving the boat past the paddle, as if the paddle is anchored in the water.

Lifelong Kayakers

After years of kayaking, your body can be subject to an alternate constellation of aches and pains. Even paddlers who have the perfect stroke, may suffer from ailments resulting from postural changes.

Flatwater sprint kayaker Maggie Hogan of team USA Canoe/Kayak. Imagine a set of Scotty rod holders on that ride!

Stretching and core strengthening can help in the long run. And that's where a lasting relationship with a physical therapist or sports trainer is every bit as valuable as that first interaction with a kayak instructor.

Michael Rosenberg is a physical therapist at Presbyterian Sports Medicine in Charlotte, NC. His office provides injury-prevention programs at Olympic training camps, medical coverage at trials, and on-site injury assessment at competitive venues. Also, Presbyterian's rehabilitation center provide cares when the Team U.S.A. athletes are in town.

"Paddlers tend to develop hip tightness, because of the sitting posture," Rosenberg said. "We see range-of-motion restrictions that affect the low back.

"We also see midback posture changes; a lot of them develop a certain posture, similar to people who work on computers at a desk all the time.

"And then some will have neck issues, as the neck may be compensating for low back and upper back posture."

Some paddlers also have nagging shoulder injuries (especially the whitewater types) which can result in limited range of motion, with cascading consequences for the body.

Rosenberg's team designed a maintenance regime for elite athletes, focusing on stretching, mobility work, and corrective work—corrective referring to the kinds of muscle imbalances which can result from kayak workouts.

Before implementing the regime, Rosenberg saw "patterns of restrictions, and bad posture" in a group of elite-kayakers ranging from 17 to 34 years in age. "Some of the younger ones couldn't do the movements the older ones could. It's possible to age with wisdom, taking care of your body."

As I talked with Rosenberg and Kettler, I realized that the two groups of paddlers actually meet: The new paddler is taught to focus on proper technique, the advanced paddler is taught to correct for lasting muscle imbalances.

"Kayaking is definitely a great sport," said Rosenberg, "But to go from the office chair to paddling on weekends, sitting up unsupported, paddling for three hours, when you've been slouching ... your body might say 'Ow!'"

If you have aches from kayaking, or are thinking of starting from a sedentary lifestyle, Rosenberg advises getting in touch with a physical therapist, or a physician trained in sports medicine.

"Go and get a movement analysis, screening from a physical therapist. They're trained to look at your body, as different from someone else's body, and help you with your own comfort level. It could be as simple as a few stretches, 10 minutes of exercises, or just education."

> ## "Paddlers tend to develop hip tightness, and range of motion restrictions that affect the low back."

Strokes to Save Your Shoulders

To avoid overtaxing your shoulders and arms, sit upright, and begin the stroke with your hips, turning your chest away from the side you're paddling on.

As you power through the stroke, push through with your foot to rotate your hip back, and drive the boat past the paddle.

Blade comes up, and switch sides, again beginning with a turn at your hips.

Feeling aches and pains after a day on the water? Have an instructor watch your strokes, and a medical professional examine your range of motion. Keep your kayaking pain-free so you can concentrate on fishing!

Paddlecraft World Records

Think you've caught a record-size fish? As a kayaker, perhaps fishing by yourself, there are some special considerations you should be aware of.

The International Game Fish Association (IGFA) maintains record categories in various metric line-classes, from 1 kilogram to 60 kilogram, roughly equivalent to 2-pound-test to 130-pound-test. The classes refer to the breaking strength of the line. Also,

Australian kayaker Mark Hope landed this 52-pound, 3-ounce barramundi on 2-pound-test line, for an IGFA line-class record. He was fishing in Lake Tinaroo in September 2011, and casting a Z-Man SwimmerZ.

there is the All-Tackle category, largest fish caught on any class of line up to 60 kg/130-pound-test. And when they say breaking strength, they mean it—with the paperwork for your record submission, you must send to IGFA, intact, the entire leader and attached 50 feet of the line. The IGFA will test the line to see its actual breaking strength.

Modern anglers are sometimes surprised to learn that "8-pound-test" braided line, for example, tests out at 12 or even 16 pounds. Thus some familiarity with the IGFA records for your favorite species, as well as fishing lines, is worth your research, if you're serious about trying to get your name in the book.

Also note that you must weigh the catch on a certified scale, one that's been certified/checked for accuracy within the past year. Does that mean you have to kill the fish? Not necessarily— the IGFA may approve a live-release catch which was weighed on "terra firma" (shore, standing on a flat, etc.), and some portable scales (i.e. Boga Grip) can be certified in advance, or after a record submission has been prepared. You'll need to take photos of the catch, the rod and reel used, the scale used, and the angler. It's best if you have witnesses.

For fish which may be subject to possession restrictions, consult state authorities before you haul them ashore for weighing.

The IGFA also has a new All-Tackle Length Class category, which takes the scale out of the picture, and accords recognition for a fish's length when measured with the official IGFA measuring device. That makes it easier to release the fish.

What about kayak-specific records? At present, IGFA has no separate record category, but the records coordinators at the Dania Beach, FL, headquarters are beginning to note some submissions from paddle anglers, including the photograph at left. The barramundi was approved as a new line-class record, taking about 5 months for the approval process.

The IGFA website, www. igfa.org, has more information, and the annual print publication, IGFA World Record Game Fishes, is a treasure trove, well worth the annual IGFA membership. The association is also instrumental in advocating for fisheries conservation and sportfishing.

Sport Fish for Kayakers

Gray Snapper
(Lutjanus griseus)

◆**A.K.A.** Mangrove Snapper

◆**Range:** Gulf of Mexico and Western Atlantic as far north as Cape Hatteras; also much of Caribbean.

◆**Size:** Common at 1 to 3 pounds. World record 17 pounds.

◆**Diet:** Shrimp, small fish

◆**Kayak Tactics:** Drift over rocky bottom or artificial reefs and fish light bucktail jig tipped with bit of shrimp or scented bait. Where current is light, or where safe anchorage is available, bottom-fish with live shrimp or pinfish steak on sliding sinker rig. Also common around docks and undercut mangrove shorelines, in South Florida.

Juvenile gray snapper (a.k.a. mangrove) hang near structure.

Glossary

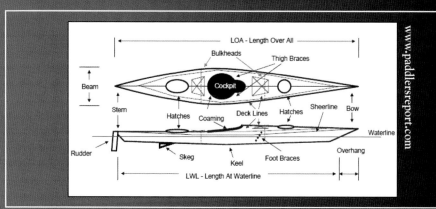

Aft – Area of kayak behind the paddler, generally, as in aft deck

Anchor Trolley – Ring mounted on a line running from bow to stern, with pulleys; may be adjusted to move anchor or drift chute line, or rode, forward or aft

Back Stroke – To propel the kayak in reverse by placing the paddle blade aft of the cockpit and pushing its convex (forward) side toward the bow

Beam – Measurement of kayak width at its maximum point, usually in inches

Blade – Curved or (rarely) flat face of a paddle

Blow-Molded – Kayak manufactured from plastic formed inside a two-piece mold, under air compression

Bow – Front or foremost part of the kayak

Braces – Posts for your feet to rest on. Some adjustable on sliding tracks; others are molded into the kayak

Bungee (or Shock Cord) – Stretchable nylon line, often criss-crossed over tank well to hold gear. May also describe rod and paddle leashes

Capsize – Kayak rolls over on centerline; paddler and his fishing gear enter water

Chine – Edge where the bottom of the hull meets the sides

Cockpit – Space in the kayak where the paddle sits

Drift Chute (also Sea Anchor) – Collapsible fabric that opens in the water to slow the rate of drift, often for fishing open bays or to offer extra drag when fighting large fish

Eyelets – Nylon or stainless steel tie-down points for seats and other kayak accessories. Usually riveted

Feathered paddle – Paddle in which the blades are fixed at an angle to each other; helps slice through the wind

Fishing Kayak – In shop vernacular, usually indicates kayak has been outfitted with rod holders and possibly other accessories

Foot Well – Recessed area of the kayak where your feet rest

Forward (or fore) – Area of kayak in front of paddler, as in fore deck

Forward Stroke – To propel the kayak forward by placing the paddle blade in the water forward of the cockpit and pulling its concave (scooped) side toward the stern

GPS – Global Positioning System. Convenient means of navigation, as long as you have power supply. Bring compass for backup

Grab Loops – Handles affixed to the kayak at bow and stern, and astride the cockpit, to ease carrying

Ground Swell – Powerful ocean waves which break on shore at regular intervals, sometimes with little or no wind

Inserts – Threaded brass fittings permanently mounted during the rotomolding process, providing a secure, water-tight attachment point for accessories

Keel – Bottom center line of the kayak

Knot – Rate of movement, as of vessel or wind, equal to 1.17 statutory miles-per-hour

Low-Head Dam – Submerged, manmade wall in a river which allows current to flow over the top, creating a spin-cycle effect on downside, capable of trapping and drowning a capsized paddler. Avoid at all costs; watch for signs, and consult local advice on unfamiliar waters

Nautical Mile – 1.17 statutory miles; important to know when navigating coastal waters

Pearl – Unfortunate result of attempting to surf a wave (not recommended): Bow pushed down by the wave, you are catapulted

PFD – Personal flotation device (vest or inflatable)

Rocker – Description of the bend in the keel; most fishing kayaks have little or no rocker

Rotomolded – Kayak manufactured from heat-softened resin which adheres to a mold as the mold turns and rotates

Scuppers – Holes molded into the hull of a sit-on-top kayak to drain water

Sea Kayak – Specially designed kayak for long-range paddling, usually of the sit-inside variety, and outfitted with foam or inflatable flotation. Typically longer than 16 feet, and narrower than 30 inches. Not ideal for fishing

Sit-Inside Kayak – Paddler is enclosed by the hull; keeping water out of the kayak is vital

Sit-on-Top Kayak – Paddler sits on top of the kayak; water egresses through scuppers

Spring Tide – Period of strongest tidal current, usually occuring around the full and new moon

Stern – Back, or aft, end of the kayak

Strainer – A downed tree or other obstruction in a river which allows water to move through but will trap you or your kayak

Tank Well – Aft deck on a sit-on-top kayak, typically with high sides to accommodate gear and scuppers

Thermoformed – Describes kayak manufactured from (typically) two sheets of plastic shaped under heat

VHF – Very High Frequency radio. Waterproof models are available

Whitewater – Flowing water with irregularities, rated on a scale of Class I-V. Class I indicates some riffles and obstacles which are easy to avoid. More challenging waters, especially Class III and up, warrant advanced training

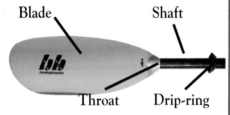

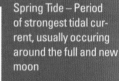

References

Want to learn more about kayak fishing? The digital world is flush with resources. The publisher of the Sportsman's Best book series, Florida Sportsman, now maintains a complete Paddle Craft Website, located at www.floridasportsman.com. The site includes daily news updates, how-to articles, blogs and robust Forums. Many of the Florida sources featured in this book are involved with Florida Sportsman Paddle Craft at various levels.

Guides and Shop Contacts

The number of kayak guide services, instructors and shops around the United States multiplies by the season, and it would be impossible to list them all in one book. The contacts below are for sources personally interviewed by the author for *Sportsman's Best: Kayak Fishing*.

California
◆OEX
Shops in Sunset Beach, La Jolla, Mission Bay
Kayak sales, rentals, trips (also diving)
www.oexcalifornia.com 858-454-6195
◆Aqua Adventures
San Diego
Sea kayak lessons, rentals
www.aqua-adventures.com 619-523-9577

California - Central Coast
◆Momentum Paddlesports
San Luis Obispo
Sea kayaking instruction, guided trips, fishing
www.momentumpaddlesports.com 805-723-4009

Florida - Gulf Coast
Matlacha Pass, Sanibel Island, Pine Island Sound
◆Josh Harvel
Inshore guided fishing
www.swflkayakcharters.com 239-233-0655
Tampa Bay
◆Neil Taylor
Inshore guided fishing
www.strikethreekayakfishing.com 727-692-6345

Florida - East Coast
Cocoa Beach, Indian River Lagoon
◆Chuck Levi, Jr.
Inshore guided fishing
www.chuckskayakadventures.com 321-302-6204

Stuart
◆South River Outfitters
Kayak sales, rentals, repairs
www.southriveroutfitters.com 772-223-1500
Jensen Beach
◆Riverfront Kayaks
Kayak sales, rentals, repairs
www.riverfrontkayaks.com 772-692-5507
Palm Beach
◆Peter Hinck
Seminars, guided fishing
561-951-2667
Jacksonville
◆Jax Kayak Fishing
jaxkayakfishing.org
◆Strike Zone Fishing
Kayak, tackle sales
www.strike-zonefishing.com 855-253-9663

FloridaTide Planning

In coastal waters of the Sunshine State, it pays to know the tides. Predictions published in newspapers and online weather sources may not account for distances between the source-station (often an inlet) and your fishing area. A hoped-for tide change may be delayed by an hour or more, if you're fishing inside a coastal bay or river. In addition to the many resources on the Paddle Craft website, Florida Sportsman prints an annual Fishing Planner, with a tide almanac for each region of the state. At right is a sample of a mixed-tide Gulf coast region, where a strong outgoing tide may follow a long day of slow-moving water. Fish icons indicate the times of strongest flows, important to know for navigation and fishing reasons alike. Time correction factors are provided for many popular spots.

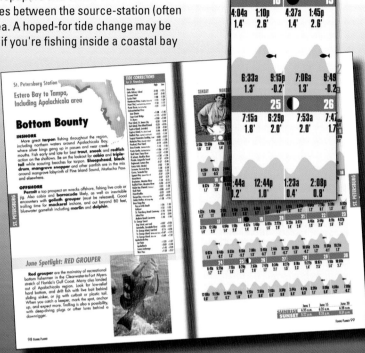

Florida Sportsman Tide Planner

Michigan/Great Lakes
◆Chris LeMessurier
Guided fishing, forums, resources
www.kayakfishthegreatlakes.com

North Carolina
◆Philip Ruckart, Yak4Fish
Bass fishing in Piedmont region
336-324-9405

Texas
◆Dean Thomas, Slowride Guide Charters
Port Aransas
Inshore fishing and Texas Kayak Fishing School
www.slowrideguide.com 361-758-0463

Washington
◆Kayak Academy, Seattle
Sea kayaking instruction, sales, community
www.kayakacademy.com 866-306-1825

International - Mexico
◆Jim Sammons
East Cape and southern California trips; kayak instruction
www.jimsammons.com 619-461-7172

Sources for More Kayaking Instruction

American Canoe Association
www.americancanoe.org (540) 907-4460

American Whitewater
www.americanwhitewater.org

World Kayak Initiative
www.worldkayak.com

River Bassin'
Website and forum for freshwater kayakers on moving water: www.riverbassin.com

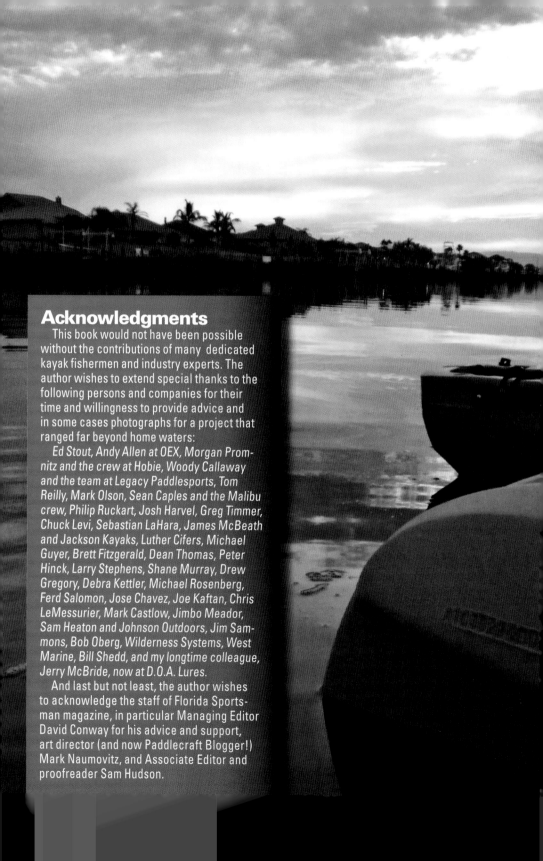

Acknowledgments

This book would not have been possible without the contributions of many dedicated kayak fishermen and industry experts. The author wishes to extend special thanks to the following persons and companies for their time and willingness to provide advice and in some cases photographs for a project that ranged far beyond home waters:

Ed Stout, Andy Allen at OEX, Morgan Promnitz and the crew at Hobie, Woody Callaway and the team at Legacy Paddlesports, Tom Reilly, Mark Olson, Sean Caples and the Malibu crew, Philip Ruckart, Josh Harvel, Greg Timmer, Chuck Levi, Sebastian LaHara, James McBeath and Jackson Kayaks, Luther Cifers, Michael Guyer, Brett Fitzgerald, Dean Thomas, Peter Hinck, Larry Stephens, Shane Murray, Drew Gregory, Debra Kettler, Michael Rosenberg, Ferd Salomon, Jose Chavez, Joe Kaftan, Chris LeMessurier, Mark Castlow, Jimbo Meador, Sam Heaton and Johnson Outdoors, Jim Sammons, Bob Oberg, Wilderness Systems, West Marine, Bill Shedd, and my longtime colleague, Jerry McBride, now at D.O.A. Lures.

And last but not least, the author wishes to acknowledge the staff of Florida Sportsman magazine, in particular Managing Editor David Conway for his advice and support, art director (and now Paddlecraft Blogger!) Mark Naumovitz, and Associate Editor and proofreader Sam Hudson.

KAYAK FISHING

INDEX

Photo Credits
All photos by author unless indicated below

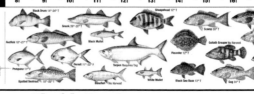

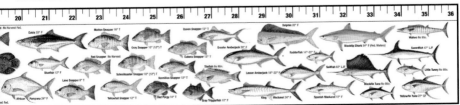

KAYAK
FISHING
DVD

The *Sportsman's Best: Kayak Fishing* DVD brings the pages of the accompanying book to life. Join author Jeff Weakley and some of the best known experts on kayak fishing as they go through the process of selecting, accessorizing, and most importantly, using and fishing from a kayak.

DVD Executive Producer: Eric Wickstrom

DVD CHAPTERS:
- ► **YOUR FIRST KAYAK**
- ► **ALTERNATIVE PROPULSION**
- ► **ACCESSORIES**
- ► **SAFETY GEAR**
- ► **TRANSPORTING**
- ► **MAINTENANCE**
- ► **OFFSHORE FISHING**
- ► **INSHORE FISHING**
- ► **FLY FISHING**
- ► **STANDUP PADDLEBOARDS**
- ► **FINAL THOUGHTS**

No matter where you live, or where you want to fish, fishing from a kayak could be your best option at catching. Read this book, watch the DVD, the rest is up to you.

"If you've ever wondered if kayak fishing was for you, this book and DVD is worth your time and money. After viewing the DVD and reading the book I'm confident your next purchase will be a kayak."

—*Blair Wickstrom, Publisher, Florida Sportsman*

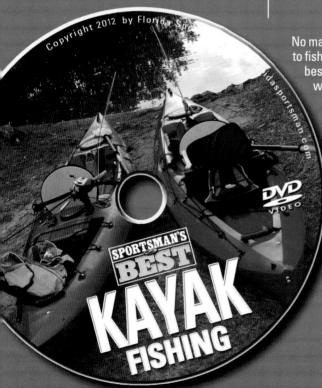

Copyright 2012 by Florida Sportsman

floridasportsman.com

DVD VIDEO

SPORTSMAN'S BEST KAYAK FISHING